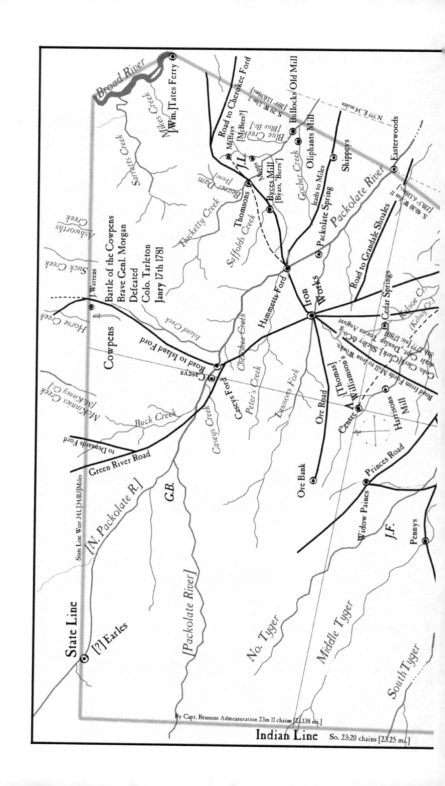

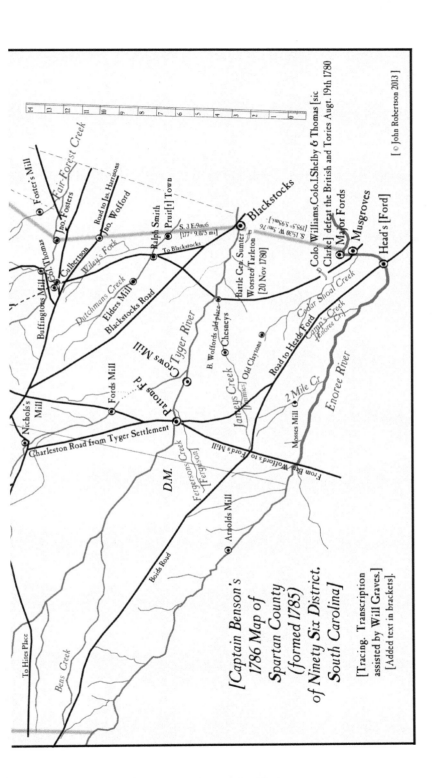

[Captain Benson's
1786 Map of
Spartan County
(formed 1785)
of Ninety Six District,
South Carolina]

[Tracing. Transcription
assisted by Will Graves.]
[Added text in brackets].

[© John Robertson 2013]

MUSGROVE MILL
HISTORIC SITE

Also by Christine R. Swager

Black Crows and White Cockades
If Ever Your Country Needs You
Come to the Cow Pens!
The Valiant Died: The Battle of Eutaw Springs
Heroes of Kettle Creek 1779-1782

MUSGROVE MILL

HISTORIC SITE

Enjoy !.

By

Christine R. Swager

Christine R. Swager

Maps by John Robertson

Illustrations by Dwight Ellisor

ISBN 978-0-7414-8344-7

Printed in the United States of America

Published April 2013

INFINITY PUBLISHING
1094 New DeHaven Street, Suite 100
West Conshohocken, PA 19428-2713
Toll-free (877) BUY BOOK
Local Phone (610) 941-9999
Fax (610) 941-9959
Info@buybooksontheweb.com
www.buybooksontheweb.com

CONTENTS

ACKNOWLEDGMENTS

I am blessed with many friends who are interested in the Revolutionary War and are always willing to help when I attempt to tell the story. I am indebted to them all as this would not have been possible without their help.

First, Brian Robson, Park Manager at Musgrove Mill State Historic Site, has been invaluable in this endeavor. He has provided sources, his own research and advice and has read and offered assistance as the manuscript progressed.

When my interest in this project was known, Will Graves, author of **James Williams: An American Patriot in the Carolina Backcountry** and **Backcountry Revolutionary** sent me the material he had accumulated in his research. This included notes, photos, Draper correspondence, and muster rolls. In addition, he directed me to pension applications on the:

revwarapps.org

a site to which he contributes. He also took the cover photo of Ron Crawley and his horse, Missy. I appreciate his generosity.

John Allison sent me primary and secondary sources on Musgrove Mill which he had gathered. He also kept me informed on his search for 'battle ridge,' and the material found there.

Robert Hall arrived at my home with his cherished edition of Landrum's **Colonial and Revolutionary History of Upper South Carolina** in case I would find it useful and I certainly did. I appreciate his thoughtfulness.

i

The prologue was read by Lamar Nelson, Distinguished Archaeologist of 2012, whose avocation is researching the early Indian history of this area. He pointed out errors in the manuscript and contributed information for which I am grateful.

Val Green answered questions about the early Indian habitation along the Enoree and Joe Epley and Tony Zeiss fielded questions I had about material they had researched for their books. Sheila Ingle interrupted her own writing to proof my manuscript.

Dr. George Fields read the manuscript and made important corrections as well as contributing his research on the battles leading to the Wofford Iron Works.

As I have for all my previous work, I enlisted the help of cartographer John Robertson who developed the maps I needed. The map of Spartanburg County is of sufficient resolution that the smallest detail is readable with magnification. John also supplied others from his collection of Revolutionary War Maps, and directed me to sources which he thought would help enrich the story. John, truly a Renaissance Man, is a tireless researcher who is generous with his talent and I appreciate his friendship. Those interested in his extensive map collection may find it at:

Global Gazetteer of the American Revolution
gaz.jrshelby.com

An afternoon in the Union County Museum with Ola Jean Kelly, Executive Director, resulted in the plats of the Musgrove holdings. It also produced information on cemeteries where Revolutionary War soldiers, many who fought at Musgrove's Mill, are buried.

As he had done for my previous book, Dwight Ellisor provided the drawings and the photos needed to illustrate the narrative. I am fortunate to have the friendship of this talented artist.

My neighbor, Julian Foster, responded swiftly to my frantic call for help with formatting and I appreciate his help.

As usual, the staff at Infinity has been helpful and gracious and smoothed the rough edges of the work.

In spite of the help of my many friends, I am certain that errors still persist and I take responsibility for them.

The purpose of this book is to provide as much material as possible concerning the Musgrove Mill State Historic Site. The site is rich in history and tradition and I have attempted to provide as much as possible.

The reader will certainly be aware that there are many discrepancies in the reports of what happened at the battle. The participants interpreted what they experienced and what they remembered. At a time when many were illiterate, we are grateful to those who dictated their stories to support their pension applications. There has been no attempt to correct their punctuation, grammar or spelling in the quoted text. Participants who wrote of the battle many years after the fact cannot be faulted for any discrepancy. The details of the battle may vary, but that does not diminish its importance.

In the early days, properties were named for their owners. Thus, the names were possessive such as Musgrove's Mill and King's Mountain. Recent usage has dropped the possessive apostrophe. However, since we are referring to early times, often I have retained the possessive.

My husband has been a patient supporter of my involvement in this project. It could not have been accomplished without his help.

Christine R. Swager
Moore, South Carolina
February 2013

INTRODUCTION

The battle and the people that lived, worked, and fought around Musgrove Mill deserve a good book, and I'm thankful to Chris Swager for her research and the excellent ways her book makes people and events come alive. You will enjoy your reading for she is a great story teller. The reader will also learn much about the region and about the people who fought the American Revolution in the Carolina Backcountry and how this little battle helped change the course of history. The people in these events are so strong, daring and unique, one might suspect a novelist created them out of a vivid imagination, but their fantastic record is well founded on sound research.

The area around Musgrove Mill has a meaningful history as a cultural and business center long before and well after the Revolutionary War battle was fought in August 1780. Native Americans lived and worked round the shoals centuries before the European settlers came. The site's natural resources- good drinking water, fertile land, water power, and the rocky shoals where trading paths crossed the Enoree River- have provided a good life for many generations over thousands of years. Some evidence of Native Americans living on the site still remains including the name "Old Indian Field," the Colonial militia muster ground for the Upper Ninety Six District in the early 1700's.

The one signal event that makes the Musgrove Mill area a more significant place in our history than hundreds of similar sites was a Revolutionary War battle fought in August 1780. This battle is one of the most unique in our Revolutionary history. The American force was cobbled together by three militia colonels from three different states, and they did not designate an overall commander. It certainly is one of the few, if not the only, battle led by a committee.

The original American plan was to raid the British fortified camp and hospital located around the Musgrove plantation and mill. After riding over 40 miles all night, they found on arrival before daylight that the post had been reinforced by a British provincial regiment. The Patriot force found themselves outgunned by a much superior enemy, and their tired horses forbid a retreat to safety in the foothills. Faced with such almost impossible odds, their frontier ingenuity developed a revised battle plan that turned the tide on the enemy. Few battles in the Revolution have its outstanding record of victory. Their good planning and combat skills clearly show the quality of the citizen soldiers and their leaders.

Musgrove Mill contributed more to winning American Independence than just winning a battle. For two months before this battle the people of the Carolina Backcountry had aggressively defended the area against the overwhelming invader. These battles show a fast learning curve in the military skills developed in a summer of fighting. At Musgrove we see a new kind and a much larger militia unit coming from all over the southern states networking together to defend their land. The American force here was comprised of men from what are now four states. I still wonder how such a force could get there ready to fight when all government fell apart after the British captured Savannah and Charleston.

The Patriot victory at Musgrove Mill raised the bar for future military actions on the South. After weeks of fiercely defending the backcountry against a superior invader, the Patriots went on the offense at Musgrove, and their victory increased their faith in themselves and their vision for future possibilities They assumed if we can whip the British at

Musgrove with a small force, then we can destroy Cornwallis' western corps under Colonel Ferguson, if we had a large enough army. They went home to gather stronger resources and achieved this strategic victory seven weeks later at King's Mountain.

The reader should remember that every person in the battle on both sides was American, not British. The people here illustrate how the war split the population into a civil struggle. Even the Musgrove family was divided between Loyalists, sometimes called by the British political name, Tory, and Patriots, sometimes called Whigs. All fighters whether a victor, killed, wounded, or captured were American with contrasting ideas about the future of their nation. In fact, the largest governmentally organized unit in the battle was the South Carolina Royalist Regiment, comprised of Loyalists from the upcountry of South Carolina.

After the battle the victorious Patriots at Musgrove continued their service in nation building. Although many of them would be considered teenagers today, they went on serving the new nation in outstanding ways. Out of this force of about two hundred, many national leaders emerged. Two served later as governors of Georgia and Kentucky. Four served as Congressmen from Georgia, North Carolina, and South Carolina. From these young officers and men in the ranks, six rose later to serve as Generals. If one clearly sees through the smoke and destruction of the battle, you can see a great nation emerging by the work of its people.

My love affair with the Musgrove Mill State Historic site goes back almost a half-century. My first visit grew out of admiration for the Patriots that I gained in reading about the battle near the mill. This admiration compelled me to put "boots on the ground" and see where and how they fought. Back then the site was very different. The Musgrove house, although deserted, was still standing. The old fields, forest, and roads were then deserted. The old monuments gave the place an eerie feeling, as if it belonged to ghosts of the past.

Much later in 1997, after my retirement from professional duties, I had more time to look over my old notes and photos of battlefields collected during my hobby years. The Musgrove Mill file caught my fancy again, and I visited the site. Walking over the area raised emotional alarms that its great historical meaning was slipping away. Although the state had purchased 260 acres of land in the 1976 Bi-Centennial, the Musgrove house had been burned by vandals and many of the old monuments were gone. When I visited the hill where old monuments on my previous visit described where the battle was fought, the monuments were gone, the land cut clear of timber, and for sale signs posted to sell lots for mobile homes. A troubling reality hit me that if we can lose a historic battlefield in a remote rural area between Cross Anchor and the Enoree River, then few, if any, of the 250 battles and skirmish sites in South Carolina are safe from neglect and development. The ghosts of the battle recruited me to get involved and help save this field and restore our state's great heritage in winning independence.

Musgrove Mill became my basic training site in battlefield preservation. Since I knew very little about preservation, I approached it as a military exercise with a mission to save Musgrove Mill Battlefield. I figured if the participants could march over 40 miles behind the British lines to raid a fortified camp, face an enemy twice the size they expected, inflict more causalities on the enemy than in their ranks, and retreat in a forced march for two days to avoid capture behind the lines, we should, could, and somehow would do the hard tasks of saving the battlefield.

A strong task force of public agencies, non-profits, businesses, and contributors assembled together to not only save this battlefield but also to open an interpretative park to the public. The task force researched the history, planned property purchase, and raised the funds to purchase the 38 acres containing the battlefield to be added the state land already purchased. The State Park Service and Palmetto Conservation Foundation led the effort, but scores of modern patriots worked and contributed in many ways. With the gift of the battlefield area, the state responded by creating a new state park, Musgrove Mill Historic Site. This book details how the preservation and park efforts were done.

I still look on this effort as a watershed in how South Carolina's extraordinary role in winning American Independence is being recognized, interpreted and preserved. The persons, businesses, and organizations that helped to save the site and open its interpretation to the public illustrate how the values of courage, sacrifice, sound planning, and hard work that created a meaningful history, still live and create good in America. The troubling thought comes in remembering that hundreds of Revolutionary War sites are threatened by development and will be lost unless we save them.

I'm thankful that Musgrove Mill battlefield and its participants set me on a new career in the latter period of my life. Enjoy this fine book. As you read it, remember and feel some of the strength of those early leaders and fighters. American Independence did not come easy anywhere, and this is clearly true for the Carolina Backcountry. My hope is that we all recover more of the American spirit and values seen in those who helped create our great nation.

George D. Fields
Chaplain (BG) USA RET

PROLOGUE

When the first white settlers moved to the site on the Enoree (EN-or-ee) River which we now know as Musgrove's Mill, they could not have known that the area had been visited by other humans over the past several thousand years.

Millions of years ago, when South Carolina was being formed, a range of great mountains rose. These mountains were higher than any on earth today and geologists call them the Ocoees (o-CO-ees). As these mountains eroded they became the red clay hills of Georgia, South Carolina and North Carolina (Savage, 1968:9). After 300,000,000 years another great range was formed to the west, the Appalachians (ap-pal-ACH-ans). The runoff from the new mountains etched their way through the now lower Ocoees and formed the river systems we know today. One of those rivers is the Enoree, a river which is of interest to us.

As the lower part of the state was inundated with the waters from the rising and falling seas over millions of years, the water came only to the edge of the foothills, to what we call the fall line. This is the line where the waters from the rivers 'fall' in the last drop before the rivers become slow and winding through Carolina's low country. During this period the rivers of the backcountry of South Carolina, including the Enoree, flowed fast and free.

Exactly when humans arrived on this continent is unclear. It was only in the early twentieth century (c 1930) that evidence was found at Clovis, New Mexico, to establish that a group of hunters occupied that area at least eleven thousand (11,000) years ago. A projectile point was found

1

imbedded in the skeleton of a mammoth, a prehistoric elephant-like animal. Subsequent evidence supported the early finds. Scientists refer to those early hunters as Clovis people and the period as Paleo-Indian. The points were attached to shafts and thrown as these people lived long before the introduction of bows and arrows. These distinctive fluted projectile points, known as Clovis points, have been found in South Carolina supporting the contention that this state has been the site of human habitation for over eleven thousand (11,000) years. Whether there were humans in South Carolina before that period has not yet been determined with certainty, but the research is ongoing (Goodyear, 2003).

Clovis Point Illustrated by Dwight Ellisor

These early people used stone tools and bone tools. The sites contain camel, horse and bison bones. The life style has been described as hunter-gatherer. These people moved to find food and sources of flint or chert which they used for their tools. The sites located in the southeast are usually on a ridge overlooking a stream and contain fluted points, scrapers and other tools which are assumed to have been used to butcher game (White, 2002).

About 10,000 years ago large animals had disappeared and herd animals such as bison and deer became an important food source. Hunters adapted to the requirements of the new prey. To distinguish this life style from the Clovis hunters, these people are known as Archaic Indians.

The period in which these Archaic peoples lived is divided into three stages.

Early Archaic Period, 10,000-8,000 years ago.

Now modern animals were on the scene. The sea level was about 100 feet below what we see today but would rise during the period. Archaeologists have concluded from the evidence that the diet of these people now included berries, seeds and nuts. Although the projectile points changed, other tools such as knives and scrapers changed little from previous times. Stone tools have been found on these sites as well as bones of deer, squirrel, turtle and shellfish. Shell middens (piles) along coastal Carolina attest to the inclusion of shellfish in the diet. However, with the lower sea level, much more coast was exposed. At the present time that coast is under water so the probable sites from that area are inaccessible. That these people traveled extensively is well documented by the distribution of artifacts found at the numerous sites which have been studied in South Carolina.

Middle Archaic Period, 8,000-5,000 years ago.

In this period the climate became more like that of today, and the vegetation would be quite familiar to us. In addition to chert, quartz became increasingly used in tool making. The stone tools found, such as axes, are more smoothly polished and more sophisticated. Engraved bone pins have been found, and soapstone slabs which may have been used in cooking. The people who traveled in South Carolina probably moved with the harvest. The oaks and hickory trees would produce nuts in the fall which would attract deer (Clement, 2008:12-13). Hunters would take advantage of the movement of deer as well as use acorns and hickory nuts in

3

their own diets. The remains of camps in South Carolina indicate that they were temporary sites used over generations.

Late Archaic Period, 5,000-3,000 years ago.

At the beginning of this period soapstone quarries were utilized in what is now Spartanburg County, close to the confluence of the Pacolet River and Lawson's Fork Creek. The soft stone was easily carved out to form bowls using bone and stone tools. Some items, which were not completely separated from the rock, are still found in the quarries. Those quarries are protected within the Pacolet River Heritage Preserve in Spartanburg County, South Carolina. Other sites from this period produce bone tools. Middens (piles) containing mollusk shells document that part of their diet. Pottery shards indicate the beginning of pottery rather than the heavier stone vessels. The first pottery was very plain and later was reinforced by fiber such as grass or Spanish moss which would stabilize the clay. The oldest shards indicate that the plainness was followed by decoration. The first decorations were merely holes pushed into the soft clay. Later the decoration is described by scientists as 'stab and drag,' a process which made a hole and then a wavy line. Clay cooking vessels were first identified in Georgia, then in South Carolina (White, 2002). Sites suggest that groups may have been less mobile and had semi-permanent dwellings. Some archaeologists define the end of this period as the beginning of limited agriculture.

Petroglyphs have been found in the mountains of South Carolina. They include both abstract designs and representations of human forms. Since the environment in which they were found is inhospitable as a living site, it is assumed that those who made the petroglyphs were visitors to the site. If so, they may have been humans who moved across the state to hunt game and gather fruits, seeds and nuts. Whether the petroglyphs are ancient, or of more recent production, is uncertain. Carbon dating requires organic material and no organic material has been found associated with the sites. However, investigation and study of the site are ongoing (Charles, 2010).

Early Woodlands Period, 3,000-2,000 years ago.

Eventually our early inhabitants cleared land to plant corn, squash and beans. This made it possible and necessary to live in more permanent, or at least semi-permanent, villages. While the Archaic sites are usually on high ground close to a water source, Woodland sites tend to be along river banks. Pottery became more decorative and was marked with fabric patterns. Stone-lined cooking pits and oval storage bins for acorns, walnuts and hickory nuts have been found at these sites (White, 2002:43). A few small burial mounds have been found in coastal Georgia and others may exist but overlooked because of their small size.

Middle Woodlands Period, 2,000 -1,500 years ago.

With more permanent villages, people apparently had time to develop more complicated social and cultural practices. Moundbuilding became more complicated, and artifacts found at sites included copper used to fashion purely decorative objects (White, 2002). Lamar Nelson, an avocational archaeologist who concentrates on Native American history, has found artifacts in Abbeville County, South Carolina, which were fashioned from material that came from North Carolina and Tennessee. Since those products are not found locally, it is assumed that the people traded and/or traveled widely. Nelson suggests that the early people were not unlike us in that they traveled to find what they liked or what worked best (Lamar Nelson Correspondence).

Although small burial mounds had been dated at an earlier period, the mounds of this period are larger and differentiated. Some mounds seem to be purely for ceremonial purposes, while others are burial mounds.

Late Woodlands Period, 1,500-1,000 years ago.

Archaeologists are finding increasing evidence that the inhabitants of this area were influenced by other cultures, specifically those of the Florida Gulf Coast and the Ohio River (White, 2002:56). Burial mounds revealed a complex ritual of including mortuary vessels, effigies of humans and animals. The burial mounds suggest that there was a social ranking among the inhabitants with the graves of the elite being more intricate than others (White, 2002:62). Although there are large mounds in Ohio dated to this period, the mounds in South Carolina are small in comparison.

Although most research on the Woodland sites in the southeast has been at sites in Georgia, there are Woodland sites in South Carolina. Frierson's (2000) study of mounds in South Carolina documents the existence of 16 mounds from the Woodlands period and speculates that there are others as yet undiscovered. His research also identified many sites which had been destroyed by plowing and bulldozing for agricultural purposes or for road fill.

Mississippian Period, 1,000-500 years ago.

The Mississippian Period, named for the Mississippi River where the first sites were identified, is characterized by the increasing complexity of the mounds and the artifacts. The most elaborate mound in the south east is found on the Ocmulgee River near Macon, Georgia. The site is maintained by the National Park Service, and contains a ceremonial earth lodge (White, 2002:67). The mound is dated at 1000 A.D. which puts it at the beginning of the period.

The mounds of the Mississippians were often clustered and appear to have been constructed within permanent communities, often with palisades for protection. Their agricultural practices became increasingly more sophisticated. Some mounds were, as with the previous peoples, burial mounds but others were built as a base for a temple for ceremonial use. Artifacts collected at sites excavated in Georgia indicate artistic motifs.

"Grave goods included ceremonial weapons and ornaments from costumes. In the latter category were copper-covered earspools, and engraved shell gorgets; necklaces and pendants of shell; cooper-covered wooden beads and beaded bands on the arms and legs; the remains of headdresses; hair ornaments; cut-outs of copper, sea-turtle shell, and mice; and copper-covered wooden rattles. One such rattle was carved in the shape of a human face" (White, 2002:77).

The most accessible mound of the period in South Carolina is the Santee Mound on the Santee River in Clarendon County. The site is protected by the United States Department of Wildlife. The mound has historic significance since, during the American War for Independence, a British stockade was erected on top of the mound. It was named Fort Watson in honor of the British commanding officer, Lt. Col. John Tadwell Watson, who built and commanded the fort. It was one of a complex of mounds but there is little remaining of the others in the area as they were used for road fill for the nearby interstate highway.

Frierson (2000) concluded that there are 19 temple mounds from the Mississippi period extant in South Carolina. Although many have been leveled and some eroded by the rivers on whose banks they were built, others are on private property and are fiercely protected by their owners. It is hoped that further study will tell us more about the purpose of the mounds.

"Just across the Broad River, at the location where the Enoree enters that large drainage, are remains of a Mississippi mound. The structure was excavated by the South Carolina Institute of Archaeology and Anthropology in the 1980's. Aside from confirming its origin in the thirteenth century, the site proved to have been occupied up till at least the contact period between Native American groups and the European deerskin traders, who infiltrated the region in the first decades of the eighteenth century" (Val Green Correspondence).

Some of the mounds along the Santee-Wateree River systems are believed to be associated with Cofitachequi, a community which was visited by the Spanish under DeSoto in 1540. Fagan reports that *"the first European missionaries to work among them (the early Indians of the south) recorded dimly remembered folk memories of moundbuilding in earlier centuries"* (Fagan, 1987: 247). Since the Mound Builders were still in South Carolina at Cofitachequi when the Spanish arrived, why do we not have information about them when the pre-historic and historic periods came so close to contacting each other?

When botanist William Bartram toured western Carolina and Georgia, he found Cherokee Indians living among the mounds. The Cherokees disclaimed any knowledge of the builders and Bartram concluded that the Mound Builders were a different people, now gone, and the Cherokees had moved into the area. Scientists now consider that the Mound Builders may have been the ancestors of the Native Americans that the European settlers encountered in the eighteenth century. How could the connections have been lost?

John Lawson may have answered the question in his journal of his trip in 1701 up the Santee-Wateree River system into North Carolina, and then down the Pamlico River to the coast. He visited Indians along the Santee and commented that there were few left. He writes that when the Europeans, Spanish, French and English arrived on this continent, they brought with them diseases to which the local inhabitants had no immunity: measles, syphilis, pneumonia, smallpox, common cold, and others (Lawson, 1709). Those diseases spread through the local population in great epidemics, decimating whole tribes. DeSoto's soldiers in 1540 had reported villages where there were great numbers of dead and dying from epidemics. Is it possible that those who knew the history of their people all perished in these great epidemics?

We will never know the cause of the missed opportunity to know about these people. We do know that they were here in South Carolina living along our rivers such as the Enoree. The abundant evidence of their lives is tangible and provides archaeologists artifacts which document their hunting weapons, their cooking utensils, their diet and their movements. This evidence is important and must be preserved and studied to recreate as much of the story as possible. However, there is no way of knowing about their family units, their social structure, rituals and spirituality. Those stories are lost.

While we lament the loss of information about our South Carolina pre-history, we are reminded that it is important that we document our more recent history. It is the purpose of this book to examine a place, the people involved and the events which took place there. The place was the site of an important battle in the Revolutionary War but was abandoned and almost forgotten for over two hundred years. At the end of the twentieth century historians, preservationists, local residents and legislators cooperated to restore and document this important history. The place is Musgrove Mill State Historic Site on the Enoree River in South Carolina.

CHAPTER ONE

The Europeans Arrive

Spain and France claimed the area which is now South Carolina but their early settlements did not flourish and were abandoned. Later England claimed the territory and successfully colonized this state.

In 1665 the King of England granted a charter to the Lords Proprietors of about 850,000 square miles, the Province of Carolina (Edgar, 1998:1). The original grant included all the land from between 36°30', the boundary with Virginia, and 29°, the border of Florida claimed by Spain. Since there was no recognized western boundary, the land literally extended to the Pacific Ocean.

The first colonists settled along the coast, and the center of the new colony was Charleston. The intent of the early settlers was to make money and rice became the source of the new wealth. However, the cultivation of rice was labor-intensive and slaves were imported to build the dikes, plant and flood the fields and harvest the crops.

In addition to the rice culture, trade in the backcountry flourished as traders moved inland to profit from the trade in deerskins with the Indians. The traders traveled along the old Indian trails, one of which used the ford that crossed the Enoree River.

Illustration by Dwight Ellisor

At the time of the Indians Wars (1711-1720) some Indians moved from North Carolina into South Carolina for their protection. One of these groups was the Eno who settled, for a time, along the river and, adding "ree" to their own name, the Apache word for river, renamed it the Enoree, the River of the Eno (Val Green Correspondence). When the danger abated, the Eno moved back to North Carolina, but their name for the River survives although the river for a time was called the Collins River after a later settler (Val Green Correspondence).

As the coastal rice culture thrived, the white owners were greatly outnumbered by the enslaved work force and became uneasy about the possibility of a slave uprising.

In addition to the threat of slave revolts, the early settlers faced other difficulties. In the interior of the colony the thriving fur trade with the Indians posed problems. The Indians, accustomed to traders who were transitory, resented the intrusion of settlers in land they had considered their own and there had been Indian attacks against even coastal areas.

Further, the Spanish presence in Florida and the Caribbean posed a threat to British shipping as well as to the coastal colonists. These residents feared that an Indian attack, coinciding with a slave revolt, would give the Spanish an opportunity to attempt to take back the territory Spain still claimed as its own. It was for this reason that the colonists petitioned England to establish a colony in the land to the south to provide a buffer between the Carolina territory and the Spanish, and, in addition, provide protection against the Indians. All white men between the ages of sixteen and sixty were required to join and train with the militia for the defense of the colony. Additional settlers in the backcountry would provide more protection for the coastal inhabitants.

In response to that request, Georgia was established in 1732 along the coast to the south, extending to the boundary of the Spanish-held territory. Savannah was established and the additional English settlers, as well as troops stationed in the new colony, provided more security for the southern border of South Carolina. In July of 1742 the British troops stationed in Georgia, accompanied by Georgia militia, defeated the Spanish at the Battle of the Bloody Marsh, on St. Simon's Island, Georgia, ending the Spanish threat to Carolina.

South Carolina had early become a sanctuary for those suffering from religious persecution. In 1680 French Huguenots, Protestants who had been persecuted by the Roman Catholic Church in France, landed in Charleston and moved up the Cooper and Santee Rivers. They became successful planters in what was then considered the frontier.

Now, wanting a buffer between the rice barons and the Indians in the back country, South Carolina gave refuge to more Europeans who were fleeing one hundred years of religious wars. The German and Swiss Lutherans had been persecuted by the Roman Catholic Church and many had fled to England. A sympathetic English monarch with German ties encouraged resettlement to America and South Carolina provided land in the interior for these refugees. The land was not profitable for rice culture, but the Europeans were farmers and artisans and soon made the area of rich farmland on the Congaree River and the upper branches of the Edisto into what became 'the breadbasket of South Carolina' (Edgar, 1998:55).

Still the threat of Indian attacks haunted the coastal settlers. King George III's Proclamation of 1763 reserved the lands west of the Appalachian Mountains from Georgia to Maine as Indian lands, prohibiting settlers from infringing on that land. However, there were Indian lands still east of the mountains: one tract was in the area of present day Greenville, and the other in the area of present-day York County, South Carolina.

The next settlers into the back country were people we refer to as Scots-Irish and they had had a long and contentious relationship with England. However, they were

Protestant, a requirement for settlement, and they were moving down along the mountains.

For centuries the Scots and English had battled along their common border. In the early 1600's England defeated the Scots and had, at that time, acquired land in Ireland in what was called the Ulster district, but is what we now call Northern Ireland. Scots were removed from their ancestral lands and forced to emigrate from their homes to Ireland.

For one hundred years the Scots lived in Ireland and those born there were considered Irish, but they retained their Scots identity. The restrictions placed on them limited their education, their ability to trade profitably or advance economically. However, it would be religious persecution which would force them to leave. The Church of England, the established church of England, wished to eliminate all who opposed their doctrine, people they referred to as 'dissenters.' The Scots in Ireland were Presbyterians, and therefore, dissenters.

The British government, supporting the Church of England, passed restrictive laws which attacked the dictates and practices of the Presbyterian clergy. This prompted over a quarter of a million of the Scots to leave Ireland in the early 1700's. Although some had landed in southern ports, most had landed in the north since the sea route from Ireland to America was shortest across the North Atlantic. Finding the areas around the ports thickly populated and expensive, the Scots-Irish moved west and, when they encountered the Proclamation Line protecting the Indian land from settlement, they turned south.

The route these new immigrants took was the Indian trail which ran along the mountains. As it became more traveled with people, horses and wagons, it became known as the Great Wagon Road, and it stretched from the mountains in western Pennsylvania to the Carolinas.

As the first of the Scots-Irish found land and settled, their children moved further south. Each year more Scots-Irish arrived in America. The influx of these refugees continued through the years until the British stopped the shipping during the Revolutionary War. The new immigrants moved to the west, and then down the Wagon Road. In 1740 they had settled western Virginia and North Carolina. About 1750 they were moving into western South Carolina at a time when the rice growers in the Charleston area were anxious for more settlers to provide a buffer between the slave holders and the Indians.

When Georgia opened new land, which had been ceded by the Indians in 1773, settlers moved into what became Wilkes County, a large area north of Augusta bordering on the Savannah River.

These new settlers in the back country of Georgia and the Carolinas were courageous, and fiercely independent. They were prepared to fight to protect and retain the land they had settled in these new colonies. Not only would they provide manpower for militia units, but would have a decisive impact on the culture and history of the Appalachian foothills. They would also play a vital role in the American Revolution.

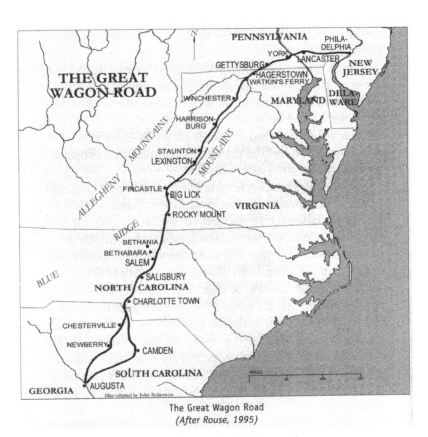

The Great Wagon Road
(After Rouse, 1995)

Prepared by John Robertson

Illustration by Dwight Ellisor

CHAPTER TWO

Backcountry Settlement

"Up to the breaking out of the Revolutionary war, the woodlands in the upper portion of South Carolina were carpeted with grass, and the wild pea vine grew, it is said, as high as a horse's back, while flowers of every description were seen growing all around. The forests were imposing, the trees were large and stood so wide apart that a deer or buffalo could be seen at a long distance" (Logan, 1897:2).

"In the year 1750, when the settlement of the upper country began, there were so many buffalos, which have long since disappeared, that three or four men, with their dogs, could easily kill four or five a day. A common hunter could kill, in the autumnal season, as many bears as would make two or three thousand *weight of* bear *bacon. The waters abounded with beavers, otters and muskrats"* (Ramsey, 1809:305).

It is little wonder that this area was soon the focus of settlement.

"The Enoree and the Tyger, for some miles above the points at which they empty themselves into Broad River, have narrow and steep valleys...early settlers found this network of small valleys with their clear streams and fertile

cane-covered bottoms unusually inviting" (Merriweather, 1940:129).

Between 1752 and 1759 about eighty men applied for land grants on the Enoree. The area was productive and there is evidence that corn was the usual crop but wheat was also grown. Mills began to appear along the rivers to grind corn and wheat. In 1755 the settlers of the area stated that they hoped to raise 'some hundreds of pounds of indigo' (Merriweather, 1940: 131). The farmers soon found that the area was well-suited to raising horses and cattle. Since the area was situated on the Cherokee path, trade was possible. Merriweather (1940:169) states that at first the guns were usually muskets but rifles began to appear by 1750 and were found frequently by 1759. This is an important fact considering the expert use of rifles in the later conflicts.

Although life was hard, the rewards of their labor made them self-sustaining. The kitchen gardens provided food for the table, and flax provided the fiber for linen, and sheep provided wool for weaving. Women spun the threads into material for clothing, often combining wool and linen into a usable fabric called linsey-woolsy. Deer hides provided leather for leggings, moccasins, and straps for furniture fashioned of wood.

The situation changed in February 1760, when Cherokees attacked one hundred and fifty settlers on Long Cane Creek. These settlers were mostly Scots-Irish, or Ulster Scots as some referred to them. Often they are referred to as Scotch-Irish. Settlements were attacked along the Broad and Saluda Rivers, and many settlers fled to the protection of the settlements along the coast. Those who stayed stockaded their homes which sheltered their families and others in the area.

"Only the stockade forts, which within a week of the Long Cane affair dotted the frontier, preventing wholesale slaughter in South Carolina.....From these rude citadels the

*men sallied out to do a little work in the fields or to look
after the cattle that were left, and in more quiet periods
families ventured to their homes. The remainder of the
population almost as far down as the fall line abandoned the
exposed regions and fled to the Congarees or farther down
the country"* (Merriweather, 1940:223).

One of these 'rude citadels' was Samuel Aubrey's Fort on
the Enoree, later abandoned for Musgrove's, two miles away
(Merriweather, 1940: 234). Musgrove's Fort, later Fort
William Henry, was the home of Edward Musgrove, but was
not at the present Musgrove's Mill site. The early
Musgrove's Fort was situated in what is now Thomas Sumter
National Forest, down steam from the present-day site on the
Enoree. Gordon's Fort was also situated on the Enoree.
Merriweather reports that the two forts on the Enoree
contained thirty-six men and nearly three hundred and fifty
women and children. In April, there was a petition from the
two forts on the Enoree reporting that they were:

*"..beset by Cherokees and weakened by the losses of
scouting parties, they declared themselves unable to hold the
forts longer without aid. They were accordingly promised a
reinforcement of fifteen men each and were warmly
commended for their long and brave defense"*
(Merriweather, 1940:227).

Responding to the desperation of the backcountry settlers,
Col. Archibald Montgomery arrived with twelve hundred
Scots highlanders in April of 1760. The troops penetrated the
backcountry but were ambushed by Cherokees and withdrew
declaring a victory (Edgar, 1998). It was certainly no victory
and the war continued.

A second British force was organized the following year
(1761) under James Grant. The British were joined by a
provincial regiment, many of whom had considerable
experience in fighting Indians. The Cherokees were attacked

in March and by June the Cherokees were routed. Villages were burned and crops were destroyed, leaving the area unable to support the Cherokees. In September 1761 the Indians sued for peace (Edgar, 1998:207).

With the Cherokee threat reduced, settlers once again moved into the backcountry.

"The bounty act of 1761 had by the end of 1765 brought into the colony about 700 persons, of whom probably 450, perhaps 500, settled in the back country...The Enoree and Tyger, with their long branches and good land, were sought by more than a hundred of the applicants, whose headrights represented about 350 persons, 60% of them appearing to be new settlers. ....On the west side below the Enoree there were a score of warrants, representing scarcely 40 headrights, less than half of the petitioners being new" (Merriweather, 1940:257-258).

The settlers were moving back to the areas which had been deserted during the Cherokee attacks. It is possible that Edward Musgrove moved into the property that is Musgrove Mill State Historic Site at approximately this time. He had previously lived at Musgrove's Fort downstream of this site and had certainly traveled this area as a surveyor. The site included the portion of the river where a wagon road crossed the Enoree River at a ford.

A typical undershot mill
Illustration by Dwight Ellisor

The shoals on the river provided an excellent location for a mill. Water was diverted to run under a mill wheel in what was known as an undershot mill. In the mountains the rivers dropped suddenly and could power an overshot wheel, so shoals were important for the location of a mill. With a wagon crossing at the ford and a mill site on the river, the location was ideal for an enterprising settler who intended to make his fortune and to provide a comfortable living for his family. Edward Musgrove was such a man.

Although the area provided a good living for the hardworking settlers, it was not without problems. Although these settlers paid taxes, they were not afforded the protection provided to the citizens along the coast. Bands of thieves, outlaws and thugs roamed the country threatening all who might have cattle and produce worth stealing. Pleas for protection fell on deaf ears in Charleston so the settlers decided to provide their own protection. They formed what became known as the Regulators.

South Carolinians were not the only backcountry settlers displeased with the lack of protection afforded them. In North Carolina the Regulators' demands were met with armed force from the Royal Governor, Lord Tyron. At the Battle of Alamance in May, 1771, the Regulators in North Carolina were defeated and the reprisals were swift and severe. Some of the Regulators were hanged and others left that area. Some moved across the mountains to the Indian Country, some moved to South Carolina and others eventually found their way to Georgia.

In South Carolina, the demands of the Regulators were ignored at first, but two ranger units were deputized to restore order to the frontier settlements (Edgar, 1998). At first the efforts were successful and the bandits were defeated or removed from the area. However, the rangers did not stop with what had been the primary goal, to restore law and order. They now targeted those whom they thought were a threat to their way of life: vagrants and idle, worthless people. *"The Plan of Regulation became the only law"* *(*Edgar, 1998: 214*)*.

Lord Acton's observation is appropriate here: ***"Power tends to corrupt and absolute power corrupts absolutely"*** (Letter to Bishop Creighton, 1887).

"With no one to challenge their authority, some Regulators took advantage of the opportunity to settle old scores. Punishment became cruel and unusual. Flogging to excess became a sadistic entertainment rather than a punishment for wrongdoing" (Edgar, 1998:214).

Violence was directed against political rivals and family enemies. Some citizens became alarmed at the excesses of punishment and sought to limit the power of the Regulators. Although some Regulators lost their authority, it became necessary to recruit settlers to oppose the extremes of the Regulators. This group became known as Moderators.

The animosity between the two groups escalated until it seemed that war would be waged between settlers. Finally, intervention by leaders on both sides resulted in a truce.

"According to the terms of the truce, both sides agreed to disband and pledged to subject themselves to legitimate governmental authority. With this reconciliation, the Regulator crisis, which had consumed the colony for two years, came to an end" (Hiatt, 2000:28).

Although armed civil war was averted, the hostility between the groups remained and those feelings would persist even through the war which was to come.

CHAPTER THREE

War Comes to the Backcountry

"The war may have begun and ended in Charleston; however, it was not won there. It was won in the backcountry" (Edgar, 1998:241).

Certainly the first stirrings of opposition to the Crown were felt on the coast. The issues which sparked the American Revolution were taxes imposed by Parliament. The financial consequences impacted merchants, artisans, shippers and businessmen located in the lowlands. The response of the backcountry would be uncertain as those settlers had more issues with the provincial government in Charleston than they did with the British (Edgar, 1998).

Sensing some Loyalist sentiment in the backcountry, Charleston sent a party of five influential citizens to attempt to assess the danger and to sway opinion to support the government in Charleston which was becoming more and more inclined to go to war to protect their independence. The five were: William Henry Drayton, Rev. Oliver Hart (Baptist), Rev. William Tennent (Presbyterian), Joseph Kershaw and Richard Richardson. It was expected that the credentials of these men would sway the settlers in the backcountry. However, William Henry Drayton was the undisputed leader of the group and he was a man of strong convictions. He assumed considerable responsibility in dealing with those who would support King George III (Buchanan, 1997).

In October, Drayton wrote a letter to Edward Musgrove asking him to pledge his support for the Patriot position. Musgrove responded:

"So you see I have interfered on neither side, only so far as you might have expected me, which I would not have come short of by any means. If I were to undertake, I would be very sorry to fail in the matter, therefore it is wisdom to balance everything in the rightscale" (South Carolina Archives and History).

Edward Musgrove would remain neutral and that would certainly be expedient. Edward Musgrove had his home and his business on the Enoree River and his mill business served the settlers of the area. The road through the back country forded the river on his property. To the north of the Enoree the Patriot sentiment was strong and the settlers would be the nucleus of the Spartan Regiment which would take the field to oppose the British occupation. To the south of the Enoree was the town of Ninety-Six which was a hotbed of Loyalist support. Musgrove's business, his family's welfare, and perhaps even their lives, would depend on maintaining the goodwill of his neighbors on both sides of the river.

The Musgrove family on the site were Edward Musgrove, and his third wife, Nancy Ann Crosby. Although the Musgrove genealogy is unclear, it appears that there were in the home children from the present and previous marriages. The son of the first wife, Edward Beaks Musgrove, was grown and it is unlikely that he lived at home. However, two unmarried daughters, Mary and Susan, both in their early twenties, were at home, as well as younger children, Rebecca, Marrey, and Hannah. These were children of the second wife and were born before 1767. The birth dates of the children of the third wife, Nancy, are unclear. Margaret's date of birth is listed as about 1771, and Leah about 1780.

No birth dates are available for the three other children, Rachel, Liney and William.

One can assume that the Musgrove family home harbored the parents, and several children. The oldest two were in their early twenties, and several girls were in their teens. Also, in the home were some younger children and possibly an infant. It is certainly not a household which could withstand attacks from their neighbors. It was expedient for Edward Musgrove to appear neutral.

The committee was met with little enthusiasm and it was evident that the settlers would prefer to be left alone. Those with strong Loyalist feelings were not persuaded, but an agreement was reached pledging that those settlers would remain neutral. However, Drayton was dissatisfied with the response of some of the more prominent Loyalists and ordered them arrested. This led to a Loyalist or Tory insurrection on 3 November 1775 when a wagon carrying arms and powder to the Indians was captured. This was followed by a Tory attack on the town of Ninety-Six on 19 November and the siege of the fort which was held by the Patriots. A truce of sorts was negotiated but was soon violated.

Drayton, now President of the Provincial Congress, ordered Col. Richardson with a force of 4000 militia and state troops into the backcountry. By the end of the Campaign, referred to as the "Snow Campaign" because of the weather, Tory resistance was dissipated.

Suffering increasing pressure from Patriot neighbors, many Loyalists made their way to British Florida and were organized into units referred to as 'Provincials.' These were men of the colonies who were trained, uniformed, and paid by the British government and were full-time soldiers. They would play a role in the conflict which was to some.

Although there was action along the border between Florida and Georgia when the British plundered the area for food for the growing population of refugees, there was little action in South Carolina. The British did send an officer, Col. Boyd, from Augusta into the interior of North and South Carolina in January 1779, to recruit Loyalist who still remained in the region. Col. Andrew Pickens with South Carolina militia followed the British recruits into Georgia and, joining Col. John Dooley and Lt. Col. Elijah Clarke, killed Col. Boyd and scattered his troops at Kettle Creek on 14 February 1779 (Swager, 2009).

In spite of the Patriot victory at Kettle Creek, the British occupied Georgia. Now entertaining the idea of sweeping up through the south in what was called the Southern Strategy, the British lay siege, and finally captured Charleston, in May of 1780. British outposts were established around the state to house British and Provincial soldiers and to provide a gathering and training post for Loyalist militia.

With no Continental Army in the South, many Patriot leaders took a parole, believing the war was essentially over. However, many resolved to continue the fight as new leadership emerged. One of the Patriot leaders who will accept a parole was Col. Andrew Pickens of South Carolina.

In July, two months after the fall of Charleston, Col. Charles McDowell of North Carolina called for the backcountry militia to muster at Earle's Ford on the Pacolet River in northwestern South Carolina. Strategically, this was a convenient location for militia from Georgia, South Carolina, North Carolina and western North Carolina, (an area now part of Eastern Tennessee), to assemble.

There was considerable opposition to the British in the backcountry. Recognizing the danger, the British had captured and imprisoned prominent citizens who opposed them. One of their prisoners was Col. John Thomas of the Spartan Regiment. He was held prisoner at the British post at Ninety-Six and was in poor health. His wife, Jane, was at the prison to take care of him. She heard the Tory women talking of a proposed attack which would take place at night

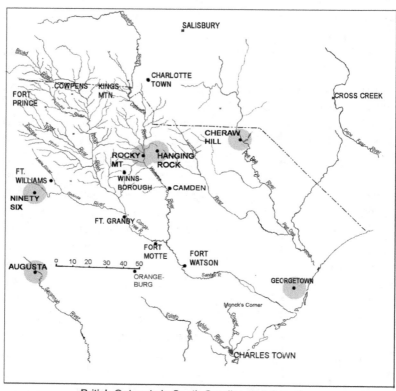

British Outposts in South Carolina and Georgia

Prepared by John Robertson

against the Spartan Regiment camped at Cedar Springs. Knowing that her son, John Thomas Jr., was commanding that encampment, she rode from Ninety-Six to Cedar Springs to warn the patriots (Hope, 2003). The distance she rode was approximately fifty miles.

On the night of 12 July, British Provincial troops, under the command of Capt. James Dunlap, moved towards the campfires at Cedar Springs prepared to saber to death the sleeping men. However, the camp was empty and the British, now silhouetted against the light of the fires, came under fire from the Patriots concealed in the surrounding woods. Dunlap's troops scattered in the dark.

Meanwhile, about three dozen Georgians from Burke County commanded by Captain John Jones, were moving towards Earle's Ford in response to Col. McDowell's call for militia. July 13 they had encountered British at Gowen's Old Fort and had captured them. The Patriots had taken the arms, horses and boots from their prisoners and sent the paroled men on foot down the road.

Captain Dunlap now realized he had Georgians in the area and proceeded to track them. It was late at night when the Georgians reached Earl's Ford and stretched out to sleep beside McDowell's Patriot camp of about 250 men. Before dawn Dunlap and his Provincials arrived at the scene. Thinking that the enemy camp consisted only of a few Georgians, Dunlap's men attacked with sabers intending to kill sleeping men. The alarm was sounded and Dunlap now realized he was outnumbered so retreated, but not before the British had killed eight Patriots and wounded thirty. One of the wounded was Captain John Jones of the Georgians who sustained eight saber wounds to the head (Hope, 2003:42).

The Patriots pursued the British and overtook them. Five British soldiers were killed in the initial attack and more were killed as the Patriots chased the enemy to the gates of Fort Prince. The Patriots withdrew and returned to camp with 35 horses, and supplies they had captured from the

British. The British evacuated Fort Prince believing that the entire militia encampment would attack.

Four engagements in four days had cost the Patriots the men killed at Earle's Ford, but had cost the British many more casualties and the loss of two forts (Hope, 2003).

Militia continued to arrive at McDowell's camp. The Wilkes County Militia from Georgia arrived, commanded by Col. Elijah Clarke. Georgia had been occupied by the British and returned to the status of royal colony. The Georgians were refugees and, having been in conflict with the British since the early days of the war, they were well aware of the necessity of resistance.

Roughly the same time, militia from what is now eastern Tennessee arrived in two groups. A small company of John Sevier's men under Major Robertson came from the Nolichucky River area. A larger group came from the Watauga River area commanded by Col. Isaac Shelby. This militia was known as Overmountain Men and they numbered here about two hundred (200).

With Gowen's Old Fort and Fort Prince now in Patriot hands, the only post offering protection for the British in the area was Fort Anderson, locally known as Fort Thicketty. On 30 July, at daybreak, militia commanded by Clarke and Shelby surrounded the fort and called for a surrender. The commander of the fort surrendered and the patriots captured 93 Loyalist militia, and a British sergeant-major, as well as 200 weapons, powder and supplies (Hope, 2003).

Clarke and Shelby moved their camps toward Cedar Springs where they were attacked by British forces.

"The battle began at daylight on August 8, 1780 where the Georgia Road forded Fairforest creek (now near the bridge of SC 295 over Fairforest Creek) and developed into a daylong battle between the British Corps of Colonel Ferguson and the Patriots under the command of Colonel Isaac Shelby of Tennessee. The morning battle continued up

the Georgia Road as it passes near the site of the first Cedar Springs battle. The larger British force was delayed all morning by the leapfrogging Patriot defensive positions along the hilly Georgia Road while the patriot leaders gathered a larger force on the high ground where the Georgia Road crossed the Pickneyville Road.

"The Battle of Peachtree. *This battle is also called Second Cedar Springs by some and Wofford Iron Works by others and took place in the present area around the intersection of Dogwood Club Road and Old Petrie Road Ext. during the midday and early afternoon of August 8, 1780. The Patriots repulsed the British and pushed the retreating enemy down the Georgia Road. In the early afternoon Colonel Ferguson arrived with reinforcements and pushed the Patriots eastward down the Georgia Road that ran along Four Mile Branch to Wofford Iron Works on Lawson's Fork Creek. In the afternoon British forces numbered over 1,200 and the patriot force around 900. From the standpoint of combatants involved, this was one of the largest battles in the upstate.*

"*Skirmish of Delaying Action at Four Mile Branch. The outnumbered Patriots fought a delaying action at about 3 PM where the Georgia road crossed Four Mile branch and set up a defensive position on the high banks at Wofford Iron Works where the Georgia Road crossed Lawson's Fork (site is located approximately 200 yards north of Country Club Road.)*

"*Wofford Iron Works. The closing phase of the August 8, 1780, daylong struggle took place along the Georgia Road took place on the high hills on each side of Lawson's Fork where the Georgia Road crossed at the Iron Works. Colonel Ferguson refused to attack the strong patriot defensive positions before nightfall. During the night the Patriots secretly evacuated their defensive positions here and retreated across the Pacolet River"* (George Fields Correspondence).

In the engagement Elijah Clarke had been wounded twice: a saber cut on the head and another on his neck. Briefly he was taken prisoner and held by two Provincials. However, seeing his son was in difficulty, he threw off his captors and returned to the fight. In this conflict, the Patriots suffered twelve casualties but had inflicted heavier damage on their enemy: thirty British dead and wounded, and fifty prisoners (Hope, 2003). In this August 8 battle, Clarke and Shelby had thwarted Patrick Ferguson, and it would not be the last time.

Col. McDowell learned that a Tory encampment had been established at Musgrove's Mill on the Enoree River. About 200 Loyalists were posted there as well as British soldiers who had been wounded in the preceding engagements. The ford at that place was convenient for use in moving military supplies from Ninety-Six to Ferguson's new position which was moved to the east and across the Broad River to protect the left flank of the British in Camden. The enlistment of Shelby's men was nearing an end but those men wanted another opportunity to engage the enemy.

Colonel Clarke and Colonel Shelby prepared to depart McDowell's camp at Smith's Ford on the Broad River. At this time, Col. James Williams arrived from Thomas Sumter's camp accompanied by Col. Brandon of the Fairforest Regiment and others, as well as men of Williams' own Little River militia. Fairforest militia came from lower Union County.

Col. Williams and his men were a valuable addition to the group. Although some of Shelby and Clarke's men may have had some knowledge of the area, these newly-arrived men were locals and knew every creek, mill, ford and settler. Now, this combined force moved to attack Musgrove's Mill.

CHAPTER FOUR

Patriot Commanders

Who were these men who rode with such haste? There were militia from western North Carolina (now East Tennessee), South Carolina and Georgia.

The perception of militia in the Revolutionary War has often been negative. Writers have referred to the militia as raw, untrained, unskilled and undisciplined. However, recent rigorous research by Michael Scoggins belies those descriptions. He writes:

"Anyone who thinks that the Carolina militiamen were useless vagabonds who rarely fired a shot in battle would do well to spend some time reading the actual records of their service" (Scoggins, 2005:158).

The militia was composed of free males between the ages of sixteen and sixty, although there is evidence that boys younger than sixteen often took part in the fighting. Future president Andrew Jackson and his brother, Robert, were thirteen and fourteen when they entered militia service. The units chose their own leaders, usually men of some stature in the area. However, prominence in the affairs of the backcountry was not a sufficient qualification for selection to the leadership role. The men chosen were trusted by their neighbors and considered to be competent leaders. All had considerable experience and the men who followed them had shared those experiences. The men who moved towards Musgrove's Mill on the night of 18 August 1780, had every reason to be confident of the abilities of the men who led them, and the commanders were equally confident of the men who followed them.

Elijah Clarke and the Wilkes County Militia

Elijah Clarke commanded the men of the Wilkes County Militia from Georgia. Clarke, a man Robert Scott Davis describes as "almost fatally courageous" (Davis, 2007), was born about 1733 in North Carolina or Virginia. He is believed to have lived at Grindal Shoals on the Pacolet River when still a teenager on property deeded to his father (Hope, 2003). If so, he was the first white settler in that area of the state. At some point he had returned to North Carolina where he married. He had been involved in the early days of the Regulator Movement in that state. However, by the time the Regulators were defeated at the Battle of Alamance in May of 1771, Elijah had moved with his family back to Grindal Shoals in South Carolina. He supported his family by hunting and trapping and trading in skins (Hope, 2003).

In 1773, Georgia acquired two million acres of land from the Indians in lieu of payment of debts the Indians had accrued. Most of this 'Ceded Land' was north of Augusta and became known as Wilkes County. Clarke was one of the first settlers when he moved into the territory in 1774. He settled at Clarke's Creek and built a cabin. The cabin, known as Clarke's Fort, was really a fortified dwelling which would protect family and neighbors from Indian attack. Although Indian chiefs had ceded the land, there was considerable hostility and the settlers had to prepare to defend themselves. When the Indian attacks came, it was Elijah Clarke who led his neighbors in retaliatory raids.

When England closed the port at Boston, the Georgians were reluctant to get involved. Their safety depends on the presence of British troops stationed in Georgia. However, when it became apparent that the British were using their Indian allies against the back country settlers, many from Wilkes County became supporters of the revolution: they became Patriots, or Whigs.

When Patriots established their control of Georgia, many who supported the King, Loyalists or Tories, fled to the safety of British Florida. With the increasing refugee population to feed, the British attacked South Georgia where there was an abundance of food and livestock. To counter this threat Patriots made three attacks against Florida, but all were unsuccessful. The Wilkes County Militia participated and Clarke was seriously wounded at the Battle of Alligator Creek.

When the British took Savannah in December 1778, the Wilkes County Militia was engaged in the battle and Elijah Clarke, wounded again in this encounter, was furious with the way the battle was fought. He understood what militia could do and what they could not do. He determined to wage war on his terms.

When Augusta was occupied by the British, and British officers were sent into the interior to recruit for their Loyalist militia, Lt. Col. Elijah Clarke, now second in command of the Wilkes County Militia, the commander, Col. John Dooly, and Col. Andrew Pickens and James McCall of South Carolina's Long Cane Militia tracked, and then attacked, the British Col. Boyd at Kettle Creek on February 14, 1779. Many historians attribute the success of that battle where Col. Boyd was killed and most of his men killed, wounded or taken prisoner, to Elijah Clarke who led his men across the swollen river to prevent the British from reforming. When his horse was shot from under him, Clarke mounted another and continued the attack, scattering the British (Swager, 2008).

However, the Patriot success was short-lived. A month later, the Wilkes County Militia was hurrying to join General

Ashe of North Carolina. The Patriot force commanded by Ashe was overwhelmed by the British at Briar's Creek. Clarke and his men arrived too late for the battle and buried the dead.

With each British advance, the men of Wilkes County retreated farther into the backcountry. When, in October, the French and American Armies attempted to retake Savannah, the militia involved was again distressed by the tactics which failed against the heavily entrenched British fortifications.

When Charleston fell in May of 1780, many militia leaders, including Col. Andrew Pickens of the Long Cane militia in South Carolina, and Col. John Dooly of the Wilkes County Militia took a parole, agreeing to lay down their arms and cease resistance. Elijah Clarke spurned the offer. He would fight to the death against the British and their Indian allies. The men of Wilkes County appointed Elijah Clarke as their commander and now, in the heat of an August night, they followed him towards Musgrove's Mill.

Isaac Shelby and the Overmountain Men

Perhaps no militia has been so maligned as the Overmountain Men who accompanied Col. Isaac Shelby on this August night. They have been described as wild as the mountains they inhabited and as savage as the Indians they fought. Major Patrick Ferguson referred to them as mongrels and barbarians. However, the history of the men of the Watauga and Nolichucky River settlements presents a picture of organization and discipline.

The first permanent settlers in what is now Eastern Tennessee arrived in 1769. They settled along the fertile valleys of the Watauga and Nolichucky Rivers. The land on which they settled was in dispute. George III's Proclamation of 1763 reserved the lands west of the Appalachian Mountains, from Georgia to Maine, as Indian lands. The territory drained by rivers flowing to the east was open to settlers, but lands drained by rivers flowing to the west were off limits to settlers. The Watauga and Nolichucky Rivers flowed into the Tennessee River and then into the Gulf of Mexico. They were clearly in Indian Territory that England was pledged to protect (Dixon, 1976).

Still the settlements grew as Virginians moved down the Holston River into the area and North Carolinians traveled across the mountains. In western North Carolina settlers, who were taxed for a palace for the royal government, protested that they were without law and order, and they rebelled. The Regulator Movement was put down when the Regulators were defeated by Lord Tyron's troops at the Battle of Alamance on 16 May 1771. Some of the Regulators were hanged, and repressive measures against the backcountry settlers were common. Seeking to escape the retribution of a vengeful royal governor, many settlers moved west into the disputed lands of Watauga and Nolichucky.

Since the settlers were clearly in Indian lands, the Indian agents, acting on behalf of the British government, tried to force them out. However, the settlers were not about to give up their homes and, since they were forbidden from purchasing Indian land, they arranged to lease the territory on which they had settled. The same year, 1772, they formed the Watauga Association, possibly the first independent governing body in the colonies. The purpose of this was to provide law and order to the settlements. Since the settlements were outside the jurisdiction of both Virginia and North Carolina, the settlers were cognizant of the possibility that their territory would be considered a haven to bandits, outlaws, those fleeing creditors and other undesirables.

The Association provided for a militia of all men over the age of sixteen to meet regularly and courts to be held in every township. The militia would have the responsibility of enforcing the law and carrying out the sentences of the courts. Those who broke the law were dealt with harshly. Horse thieves were hanged (Dixon, 1976)!

For months after the lease was negotiated, there was peace between the Wataugans and their Indian landlords. New inhabitants moved in and the increase in population provided more manpower for a well-organized militia. Although the royal governor continued to issue orders of eviction, few settlers moved.

The land to the west of the Watauga and Nolichucky was coming to the attention of land speculators and politicians. That land was Kentucky and it fired the imagination of men like Daniel Boone and other pioneers. Speculators coveted the land which they intended to procure. Then, they would sell to settlers who wished to travel to this bountiful land. To accomplish this it was necessary for the speculators to deal with the Indians.

On 1 March 1775, Indians and white men met at Sycamore Shoals for what can only be regarded as a great festival: races, feasting, etc. The agenda of many men was a purchase of the Kentucky land. The Wataugans had no interest in Kentucky but were present to forward their own agenda. They were able to purchase from the Indians the land they had leased, and more land in the bargain- a total of two thousand square miles. This was Watauga Country (Dixon, 1976).

The royal governor decreed that the sale of the lands was illegal ending, for a time, the settlement of Kentucky. However, the Wataugans were firmly settled on their land and any attempt to evict them was preempted by the events of the American Revolution.

Wataugans considered the options carefully. Should they remain loyal to the King, or should they support the Patriot cause? It was clear that the Indians would be used by the British against the settlers and, if the British won, there would be a concerted effort to remove the settlers from beyond the Proclamation Line. If the Patriots won, settlement would be encouraged beyond the mountains. The Wataugans would be Patriot! In the fall of 1775 the Wataugans declared for the Patriot cause and designated themselves as the Washington District taking the name from the leader of the Continental Army, General George Washington.

In 1776 the British attempted an attack on Charleston and the American troops called for support. In spite of being under threat of Indian attack, the Wataugans answered the call for help and sent a platoon of riflemen, commanded by Lt. Felix Walker, to the Charleston area. As the British Navy attacked Sullivan's Island (later to be called Fort Moultrie), Col. Thomson and South Carolina troops were protecting the coast to prevent British troops from landing at Breach Inlet. Although the reports of what happened there reflect widely different results, there is no disputing that the British were prevented from landing and were forced to retire. That battle ended, for the time, the British invasion of the south, and the Wataugans had been part of the Patriot victory.

However, the backcountry was far from peaceful and, after repeated Indian attacks, three campaigns were initiated against the Cherokees. Militia from Virginia, North Carolina, South Carolina, Georgia and Watauga moved into the Indian Territory burning homes, destroying crops and confiscating supplies. The Cherokee Nation was reduced to a few bands of disaffected Indians who would continue to harass the settlers of the back country.

It was advantageous to be part of the newly declared independent colonies so the Association approached Virginia and asked to become part of that colony. When they were rebuffed, they approached North Carolina. Although they had had poor relations with North Carolinians in the Regulator period, the royal governor had fled. North Carolina accepted the offer as it was in their best interest. Not only were the settlements on their western border, but the Wataugan settlements could raise six or seven hundred riflemen. With the remaining Indians acting in conjunction with the British, as well as incited to action by disaffected young chiefs, a well-established, disciplined and vigilant militia in the west was a decided advantage to North Carolina.

The British returned to the south in 1778 and captured Savannah. After securing Georgia, they moved to siege Charleston, South Carolina which fell in May of 1780. The British moved into the backcountry and attempted to secure the area for the King. When Col. Charles McDowell issued a call for militia to muster he sent word to Isaac Shelby who was surveying in Kentucky. Shelby was part of the Holston River settlements and had fought for Virginia in the Indian wars. Shelby mustered about two hundred of the men of Watauga and moved across the mountains to join McDowell. These were experienced and disciplined riflemen who had established and maintained law and order in the over mountain settlements. Recently they had been successful at Fort Thicketty and in the running battle around Wofford's Iron Works. Now, in the heat of the August night, they followed Col. Isaac Shelby to Musgrove's Mill.

Col. James Williams and the Little River Militia

The men of the Little River Militia were settlers in what are now Laurens and Union Counties of South Carolina and the man they followed was a well-known and well respected militia commander. James Williams and his wife moved from North Carolina to the Little River, a tributary of the Saluda River, in late 1773 or early 1774, where Williams soon established himself as "a farmer, miller and merchant" (Graves, 2002:7). From the beginning of the disaffections with England, Williams declared himself ready to fight for a solution. Like other settlers, he thought at first that some accommodation could be made with the Mother Country but, when that seemed impossible, Williams not only supported the cause but became an active officer in the Patriot militia. He risked everything and he had a lot to lose. Not only was he a successful businessman, but he lived in an area where support for the King was strong and vicious.

Like the other commanders on this ride towards Musgrove's Mill, Williams had a wealth of battle experience. Will Graves' research documents Williams's participation:

"in the first Battle of Ninety-Six (November 19-21, 1775), the so-called "Snow Campaign" (January 1776), the Cherokee expedition (July-October 1776), the ill-fated Florida campaign (May-June 1778), the Augusta Campaign (December 1778-January 1779), the Battle of Briar Creek (March 1779), the Battle of Stono (June 26, 1779), and the unsuccessful siege of Savannah (September-October 1779)" (Graves, 2002:16).

When the British occupied Charleston in May of 1780, many Revolutionary leaders accepted a parole which allowed then to return home if they promised not to take arms against the King. Under those conditions they would not be molested by British troops or Tory militia. Many leaders, including Andrew Pickens, took a parole. Later, the British general, Sir Henry Clinton, changed the rules and demanded that those on parole join the Tory militia and fight against their former comrades-in-arms. Many felt that since the rules had been changed, they were no longer bound by their parole and returned to the fight.

Col. James Williams, as well as his comrades on the ride to Musgrove's Mill, Elijah Clarke and Isaac Shelby, had refused to take paroles and determined to fight to the death. Since Williams was a prosperous planter in an area dominated by Tories, he certainly knew he was taking a great risk of personal and property destruction. For that reason he had, in July, moved much of his valuable property, livestock, slaves and personal belongings to the home of his brother in

North Carolina. He and his family would stay in their home in Little River and continue their business in the face of the enemy. His wife and sons would run the plantation while Col. Williams went to war. Now, on the night of 18 August, he joined Clarke and Shelby, determined to strike a decisive blow to the Tories assembled at Musgrove's Mill.

That Col. Williams and his men had left Thomas Sumter's camp to join McDowell's campaign has been interpreted by one of Sumter's officers and friend, Col. William Hill, as treachery. Hill's vitriolic attack is totally unsupported by any documentary evidence but was accepted by Lyman Draper as fact and included in his book, **King's Mountain and Its Heroes**. Other historians have repeated the claims by quoting Draper and James Williams's reputation has been tainted for generations.

Dr. Bobby Gilmer Moss is a scholar with an encyclopedic knowledge of primary source material dealing with the Revolutionary War in the south. In his more than fifty years of researching both American and British documents, he has found no evidence to support Hill's claim against Williams.

Will Graves, author of **James Williams: An American Patriot in the Carolina Backcountry**, and webmaster of www.southerncampaigns.org/pen wrote the following in response to a question of evidence from the pension applications:

"I have now finished the first cut of the SC (South Carolina) and NC (North Carolina) pension applications and I can say authoritatively that there is absolutely no mention by any pensioner of any conflict between Williams and Sumter and/or Hill. That the pensioners were not bashful about mentioning controversy among the officers is proven over and over again in their applications. The absence of any such statements in any of the pension statements is one of the most compelling arguments, I

believe, for the falsity of Hill's accusations" (Graves Correspondence).

It is not prudent to interrupt the narrative here to speculate about Hill's motivation. However, what was Williams's motivation in leaving Sumter's camp to join McDowell's campaign?

Militia, for the most part, had loyalty to their local districts and concerns for the safety of their homes and families. It should be noted that Thomas Sumter was campaigning against British troops posted in Camden. Col. McDowell was directing his attacks against troops posted at Ninety-Six.

Williams' home on Little River was between the Enoree River and the British post at Ninety-Six, about 15 miles from Ninety-Six. Col. Williams had left his wife and children at his home. In late June, troops under Major Patrick Ferguson's command from Ninety-Six occupied the home and evicted Mrs. Williams and her children and forced them to find refuge in the outbuildings at the Williams' mill. With his family under house arrest, it is little wonder that Williams returned to the area.

The men who accompanied Williams to McDowell's camp had similar concerns. Men of the Fairforest Militia under the command of Thomas Brandon were from the area which is now Union County and they, too, were concerned about the vulnerability of their homes and families to the British and Tories posted at Ninety-Six. It is safe to say that all perceived the troops from Ninety-Six as the greatest threat to their families and homes and McDowell was directing his attacks against those soldiers.

James Williams and the men who rode with him were experienced fighters with complete confidence in the man who commanded them. His reputation as a commander had been earned over the years. They were in their own territory as they headed for Musgrove's Mill.

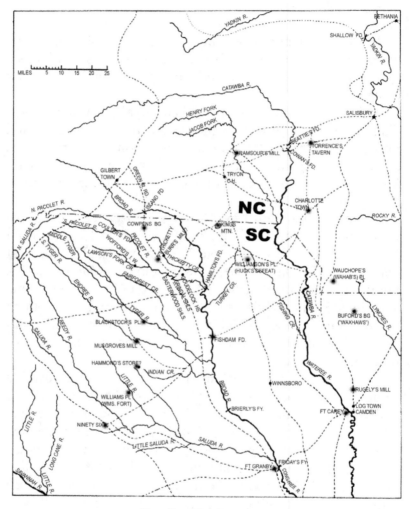

Carolina Backcountry
Prepared by John Robertson

The map above shows (in the lower left) how close
Williams' home was to the British post at Ninety-Six.

Now the combined militia of Clarke, Shelby and Williams moved towards the enemy at Musgrove's Mill. Not only were the leaders of this attack capable and experienced, many of the men who rode with them this night had accompanied them on previous campaigns, and were confident of the abilities of the men who would lead them into battle.

CHAPTER FIVE

The Enemy at Musgrove's Mill

As night fell, the three militia units moved through the woods toward the road to Musgrove's Mill. The men rode silently, aware that Major Patrick Ferguson and his British Provincials and Tories were camped to the east. When the Patriots moved onto the road, they spurred their horses and galloped south. Although there are several accounts of what happened, there are discrepancies. Shelby reports that they rode without stopping to rest or to water their horses. However, Shelby wrote the account long after the fact and possibly confused the haste of the retreat with the trip to the battle.

Hammond reports that they did stop to rest and water the horses. This is more reasonable as militia was dependent on their horses and would surely have rested and watered them as they rode through the heat of a mid-August night. They were, however, intent on the mission and would have wasted little time.

According to Hammond, they arrived near the post (Musgrove's Mill) at sunrise. Williams, Shelby and Clarke had agreed on a combined command and, not knowing the exact location of the enemy, sent out scouts to reconnoiter.

Further, the Patriots learned from a local resident that Provincial troops from Ninety-Six were camped at Musgrove's Mill. They were moving to join Major Patrick

The Enoree River

Ferguson, who had moved to the east to support Camden, and had set up an overnight camp at the site. Now, confronted with a far larger and more experienced force, and no possibility of retreat on their exhausted horses, the commanders prepared for battle.

Who were at the British Camp at Musgrove's Mill? When the Patriots left McDowell's camp they expected to find only Loyalist militia encamped there, along with some wounded from the battles at Cedar Springs and Wofford's Iron Works about ten days before. Loyalist militias, like Patriot militia, were citizen soldiers who mustered when needed. However, Loyalist or Tory militia were paid and supplied by the British so we have better records or muster rolls available on these units since the British required verification for the pay rolls.

Brian Robson, Historian and Park Manager at Musgrove Mill State Historic Site, has conducted considerable research on this topic and the following numbers are based on his deductions.

The camp at Musgrove's Mill had been recently established as a site not only to care for the wounded, but also to control movement across the Enoree River. There was a primary ford on the Musgrove property, and another, a rocky ford, was also on the property about a quarter of a mile upstream. Two others, Head's Ford two miles upstream, and Jone's Ford about eight miles downstream, allowed passage for travelers to and from Ninety-Six and Charleston to the upcountry or what is now the Spartanburg area of South Carolina.

The recent battles at Fort Thicketty, Cedar Springs and Wofford's Iron Works had not gone well for the British and the loss of Gowen's Old Fort, Fort Prince and Fort Thicketty had deprived the British of places of safety. It was important to control the roads and fortify areas used for the movement of troops and supplies. Also, a mill on site allowed troops to grind corn and wheat which were staples for all who lived and traveled in the backcountry. Musgrove's property was an excellent site for the new camp.

Who were the Loyalists the Patriots expected to find here? Col. Daniel Clary had been authorized to raise a regiment from the Dutch Fork region of the Ninety-Six District Loyal Militia. Born in Maryland in 1710, Clary was now 70 years old and had settled on the Saluda River in Newberry County in 1773. He had been a conspicuous supporter of the King throughout the unrest in the back country. When Major Patrick Ferguson, Inspector of Loyalist Militia, was authorized to form seven regiments, Col. Clary organized the Dutch Fork Regiment. The expectation was that a regiment would consist of 200 men.

The Dutch Fork Regiment was able to muster barely 100 men for service, in spite of the fact that its commanding officer, Daniel Clary had been involved in the uprising of 1775, and was highly regarded by his Loyalist neighbors.

The relatively poor record of enlistments for this regiment may have been due to the fact that a large number of men from the district had fled to Florida and returned from exile with the South Carolina Royalists, a Provincial unit (Lambert, 1987:111).

The muster rolls of Clary's militia are included as Clary-Appendix. It is assumed that most of those men would have fought at Musgrove's Mill, a number of about one hundred. Patrick O'Kelley lists the unit commanders under Col. Daniel Clary as: Captains William Hawsey, Vachel Clary, Humphrey Williamson, William Ballentine, George Stroup, James Wright and William Thompson (O'Kelley, 2004, Vol. 2: 288).

Added to Clary's militia was a detachment of David Fanning's Loyalist Militia of North Carolina numbering, according to Fanning's report, fourteen. *"I then Joined them with a party of 14 men the morning following the picketts were attacked by a party of Rebels"* (Fanning, 1865). It is unknown if any of the men who had been wounded previously were involved in the battle. However, the information the Patriots had prior to the battle led them to expect a small encampment of Loyalist militia in numbers inferior to their own.

As mentioned previously, the Patriots learned at their arrival that the camp had been re-enforced overnight by Provincials from the British fort at Ninety-Six. Once in America, Great Britain had enlisted men who were loyal to the mother country into units referred to as Provincials. These units were uniformed, paid and equipped by England and they were full time soldiers. Most had been recruited in the northern colonies, many from New York and New Jersey where the inhabitants were fiercely loyal to Great Britain. Many of these units had been transferred to the south where they now were assigned to the British post at Ninety-Six. Some were now at Musgrove's Mill.

Reports written at the time do not agree. An interesting, but incomplete, account was written by Lt. Roderick MacKenzie of the 71st Regiment (Frazer's Highlanders) who saw considerable action in the Southern Campaign. He was not present at the battle but wrote the following:

"The Americans, under Colonels Williams, Shelby, and Clarke, were strongly posted on the Western banks of the Enoree; their numbers have not been precisely ascertained, probably five hundred. The detachment of British troops, commanded by Lieutenant Colonel Innes, consisted of a light infantry company of New-Jersey volunteers, a captain's command of Delancy's, and about one hundred men of the South Carolina regiment mounted. The troops passed the river, the infantry drove the enemy at the point of the bayonet, and the horse, though but lately raised, and indifferently disciplined, behaved with great gallantry; but in the moment of victory, the commandant, Major Fraser, Captain Campbell, Lieutenants Chew and Camp, five of the seven officers present, were wounded by a volley from the Americans. The British troops, consequently unable to avail themselves of the advantages which now offered, were conducted by Captain Kerr to the Eastern side of the river, where they remained till reinforced by Lieutenant Colonel Cruger" (Mackenzie, 1787:25).

This account is interesting on several levels. The writer obviously thought this was an important encounter and was faulting Lt. Col. Tarleton for omitting the incident in that commander's **A History of the Campaigns of 1780 and 1781 in the Southern Provinces of North America**. The casualties among the British officers are recorded. However, the last entry referring to Lieutenant Colonel Cruger is in error. At a later engagement, Cruger went to reinforce Lieutenant Colonel Thomas Brown when the British post at Augusta was under attack by the Americans commanded by Colonel Elijah Clarke who had been at Musgrove's Mill. The

Augusta attack was 14-18 September. There is no evidence that Cruger was ever at the Musgrove Mill encampment. The "*about one hundred men of the South Carolina regiment mounted*" refers to the South Carolina Royalists commanded in the field by Major Thomas Fraser although Lieutenant Colonel Alexander Innes was nominally in command (Lambert, 1987:151). Thomas Fraser was a Loyalist from New Jersey whose capabilities had impressed Lord Cornwallis. A provincial unit, the Royalists had been organized in East Florida in 1778 (Lambert, 1987:71). In December of that year the Royalists had marched overland from Florida to Savannah and participated in the capture of that city (Lambert, 1987: 81), and had seen action at the Siege of Charleston. After the fall of Charleston, the Royalists were furloughed as a financial consideration. The British commanders felt they were not needed and money could be saved by the furlough.

The Royalists were recalled after Huck's Defeat at Brattonsville on 12 July (Lambert, 1987:150). Lambert reports that only about 50 of the original group mustered and the ranks had to be filled with inexperienced men. Lambert would attribute the substantial number of wounded at Musgrove's Mill to their inexperience as a unit. MacKenzie refers to them as "*recently raised and indifferently disciplined.*" However, the size of the unit at Musgrove's Mill varies with reports. Combining the reports of Lambert and MacKenzie, it is probable that there were about 50 experienced soldiers in the unit and as many again of new recruits. Robson's research supports Lambert's claim that there may have been as few as fifty experienced troopers with Fraser's Royalists.

Accompanying Col. Innes was a company of the 1st Battalion of Delancy's Brigade. Commanded by Captain James Kerr it consisted of about 50 men (O'Kelley, 2004, Vol. 2: 287). DeLancy's Brigade had been organized in New York, a hot bed of Loyalists, in September, 1776. It was named for the Brig. Gen. Oliver DeLancy whose family sponsored and supported the unit financially. Lt. Col. John Harris Cruger was commissioned to command the 1st Battalion of DeLancy's Brigade. He was a wealthy merchant with strong Loyalist convictions and married to Ann DeLancy, the daughter of General Delancy. In spite of the appearance of nepotism, Cruger was an able officer who had the confidence of the British. Their first assignment was garrison duty on Long Island.

In November 1778, DeLancy's Brigade accompanied the Campbell expedition to Savannah, Georgia and saw action at the Battle of Savannah. From February to August of 1779 Cruger was posted at the garrison at Fort Morris, on the coast of Georgia, but returned to Savannah and participated in the Defense of Savannah against the American and French forces in September and October of 1779. After the British victory Cruger's battalion remained in the vicinity of Savannah on garrison duty. In June 1780 Cruger was taken prisoner but was exchanged for the American Col. John McIntosh who had previously commanded Fort Morris before the British gained that post.

After the British victory at Charleston, the British occupied Ninety-Six as a post to give protection to the Loyalists in the area and provide a base of operations for British troops. Cruger's battalion was assigned to that post and marched from Savannah to Ninety-Six by way of Augusta. Now, in mid-August they moved to Musgrove's Mill under the command of Captain Kerr. Although Cruger did not accompany the company, these men were experienced troops who had seen considerable action in the north and in the south under the command of a very capable officer.

The 3rd Battalion of the New Jersey Volunteers was part of the force which moved into Musgrove's Mill. These were also experienced Provincial troops. Organized in 1776 in the area of New Jersey close to New York, they saw action immediately in that vicinity. After a reorganization of the regiment, the command of the 3rd would be given to Lt. Col. Isaac Allen, a Trenton lawyer. Allen would command the unit until the end of the war and he was a capable officer. One hundred and twenty of the unit were detached to serve under Captain Patrick Ferguson in a raid into New Jersey. Years later many would serve with Ferguson again, notably at King's Mountain.

In November 1778, the 3rd Battalion accompanied Lt. Col. Archibald Campbell's expedition to Georgia and fought at the Battle of Savannah. They continued to serve in Georgia through 1779. When the American and French forces sieged Savannah in September and October of 1779, the 3rd Battalion manned a redoubt on the front line and repulsed an attack by South Carolina Continentals commanded by Lt. Col. Francis Marion.

After Charleston fell, the 3rd Battalion moved to garrison Augusta, Georgia in July 1780. Shortly after they were moved to Ninety-Six. Now, in the August heat, they were at Musgrove's Mill under the command of Captain Peter Campbell. They were experienced, well-trained Provincials who had performed well in combat.

Sources vary greatly on the number of British and Loyalist troops at Musgrove's Mill that morning. American sources inflate the number of the enemy, and British sources inflate the number of attackers. What is certain is that the Patriots were outnumbered by a force which included local Loyalist militia and experienced, well-trained and well-disciplined Provincial troops.

CHAPTER SIX

The Battle

An American author, Norman Mailer, has observed that nothing can be factual. Everything is colored through the eyes of the recorder so no interpretation of events can be called 'true.' This is an important point to remember as we read the reports of the battle which vary with the narrator.

Shelby's account was written many years after the fact and he indicated that the number of men involved was *'seven and eight hundred picked men.'* Hammond's account, date unknown, refers to *'our little band,'* but the number reported in his narrative is blurred and unreadable. Williams, writing a report of the battle for the Commander in the South, General Horatio Gates, dated 5 September 1780, states :

"Col. Williams, Col. Shelby and Col. Clarke with a party of South Carolinians and Georgians in Number about Two Hundred, March'd from the North Side of Broad River on the 17th August in Order to attack Two Hundred Tories on the Innere R. at Musgrove's Mills" (Williams in Graves, 2012:196-197).

McJunkin's 1837 narrative mentions the retreat from the battle with these words:

"...knowing that Col. Ferguson whom we had just passed a little on our right, must also have heard our firing, & not

knowing but that they would break in upon us (who were only about 150 strong), & serve us worse than we did the Tories" (McJunkin, 1837).

It is likely that the number was about 200. Since Williams's after-action report was written close to the date of the engagement, that number should have been the most accurate.

Although Clarke and Shelby had mustered about 600 in previous attacks such as Fort Thicketty, Park Manager Brian Robson suggests that 200 would be a reasonable number to accomplish an attack which depended on speed, stealth and surprise. Believing that only roughly that same number of Tory militia were camped at Musgrove's Mill, two hundred would have been deemed sufficient for a surprise attack. The movement of six hundred men would have certainly aroused considerable attention.

The patrol, which had been discovered by Tories, had killed two of the Tory militia, wounded another and taken one prisoner. However, the alarm had been raised and the element of surprise no longer a possibility. With horses too spent to go further, retreat was not an option. They must fight.

Now, a frontal attack against a superior number was not feasible. The Patriot commanders ordered their men to take cover on a wooded slope adjacent to a clearing across the river from the British. Other accounts indicate that the ridge overlooked an old Indian field, a term to indicate a cleared area which Indians had, for generations, burned, cleared and planted.

How far from the river this put the Patriot line is in dispute. James Williams reported *"we drove them about two miles."* Richard Thompson, a young boy of the area, wrote *"I passed the battle ground a few days after the battle. It commenced two miles this side of Musgrove's Mill, tolerably level woods."* Isaac Shelby suggests that the distance from the battle line to the Enoree River was about half a mile. Recent excavations by John Allison have determined that 'battle ridge' is about one and a half miles from the ford across the Enoree. There the men threw up makeshift breastworks from fallen trees and brush in expectation of a British attack. According to Shelby, this was accomplished in half an hour.

To provoke the British into approaching the concealed militia line, Captain Shadrick Inman of Clarke's Wilkes County Militia lead a group of about a dozen mounted men toward the British line and fired on the enemy before retreating. This action was repeated.

Since the British and Tory officers met in the Musgrove's home, that family was privy to the conversations. They reported that the junior officers advised waiting for a British patrol to return before engaging the enemy. Col. Innes overruled the junior officers and ordered the troop to take to the field.

Hammond's account is the most complete of the action which took place:

"Thus disappointed in the hope of surprising them, it was resolved to send in sixteen well-mounted, expert riflemen, to fire at the enemy, and draw them to attack us on the hill. This was done; our horses were picketed three hundred yards in the rear, and we were formed a little upon the descent, towards the enemy. Each colonel took his station to command his own men. The sixteen sent out, were, in retreating to fall upon the left flank of the enemy, and from their horses keep up a fire upon them. As they advanced, this command was united to Captain Shadrick Inman, of Georgia- a like number placed on the right flank with the same orders. There were sixteen men left, also, as a main guard, on our horses, this reduced the whole effective force, including officers to about-------men" (Hammond, undated).

It is a great disappointment to the researchers that the number in the Hammond reported is indecipherable. He continues:

"These were placed in one line, in scattered or open order, and were ordered not to fire until the enemy were within fifty yards, and also to be governed by a single shot from Colonel Shelby; to be steady and take good aim. Being thus prepared, the enemy were drawn out. They came flushed with the hope of an easy victory, in full trot. Reinforcement had joined them the day before, of which we had no information; Colonel Innis and Major Fraser, with one hundred and fifty regulars-York volunteers-had joined the tories" (Hammond).

The "York volunteers" were the New York Volunteers, a provincial unit. The DeLancy Volunteers, which were also at the battle, were also from New York.

Hammond continues: *"They advanced in three columns--- the regulars, commanded by Major Fraser, in the center--- the militia on the right and left. Advancing, at the distance of one hundred and fifty yards, they displayed and gave us a fire, which was not returned but from our flanking parties. They then advanced with trailed arms; their columns displayed, and were allowed to come within forty yards, when the signal was given, and their ranks thinned. They fell back, and before a second fire they formed and again advanced."*

There is a story about an event which is purported to have happened about this time. Some accounts indicate that the British, with bayonets, had pushed Shelby's men from the line and that Elijah Clarke, seeing their predicament, rushed his Georgia reserves in to hold the line. Shelby's men resumed their attack with the mountain yell which later became famous as the Rebel yell of the Civil War.

Draper writes of the incident:

"A strong force, composed of the Provincials, led on by Innes and Fraser. Forming the enemy's left wing, drove, at the point of the bayonet, the right wing under Shelby from their breastwork. It was a desperate struggle-Shelby's men contending against large odds, and the right flank of his right wing gradually giving way, whilst his left flank maintained its connection with the center of the breastwork. The left wing, opposed by the Tories, retained its position, and seeing Shelby in need of succor, Clarke sent his small reserve to his aid, which proved a most timely relief. At this critical moment, as Innes was forcing Shelby's right flank, the British leader was badly disabled, fell from his charger, and was carried back-shot, it was reported, by one of the Watauga volunteers, William Smith, who exultingly exclaimed, "I've killed their commander," when Shelby rallied his men, who raised a regular frontier Indian yell, and rushed furiously upon the enemy, who were gradually forced back before the exasperated riflemen" (Draper, 1881:108).

Draper's account contains an amazing amount of detail but Shelby's account does not mention this incident. He writes:

"The Enemy had gotten within a few yards of our works: at that juncture Colonel Innes who commanded the enemy was badly wounded and carried back, and every other regular officer except one Lieutenant of the British was either killed or wounded when the enemy began to give way, just at that moment also Capt. Hawsey an officer of considerable distinction among the Tories was shot down near our lines while making the greatest efforts to animate his men. The Tories upon the fall of Capt. Hawsey broke in great confusion, the slaughter from thence to the Enoree River about half a mile was very great, dead men lay thick

et

Hammond's account relates a similar situation:

"On the second fire, they fell back in confusion. The fire then became brisk, and was kept up on our side. The tories saw the regulars fall back in disorder, and they also gave ground in confusion, and in fact without anything like pressure on our part" (Hammond).

Could the Draper story be accurate, or is it a later embellishment of the action related to Draper years after the battle? That Shelby's men uttered what Draper calls "their frontier Indian yell" is well established. Capt. DePeyster of the British force would later remark that when he heard Shelby's men at King's Mountain, he knew it would be a fierce fight because the 'yelling boys' were there. He had heard the yell during the battle at Musgrove's Mill.

Also, Clarke was known to be a fearless warrior. Shelby would later tell that he had stopped during the thickest of the fight at Musgrove's Mill, (Schenck says it was at Wofford's), to watch Clarke fight. Robert Scott Davis, the premier historian on Kettle Creek, refers to Clarke as "almost fatally courageous."

Another episode of interest which is not mentioned by the major participants is told in Draper:

"In the midst of the confusion that followed, Clarke and his brave men, following Shelby's example, pushed forth from their barrier, yelling, shooting and slashing on every hand. It was in the melee, when the British defeat was too apparent, that the Tory Colonel Clary had the opposite bits of his horse's bridle seized at the same moment by two stalwart Whigs. He had, however, the ingenuity and presence of mind to extricate himself from his perilous situation by

exclaiming-'Damn you, don't you know your own officers.' *He was instantly released, and fled at full speed"* (Draper, 1881:109).

Later authors identified the men who had grabbed the bridle as Georgians. If the incident happened, and the account has come down through the Clary family who still resides in the area, it is reasonable that the men involved were Georgians. Clarke and Shelby had been together for previous actions, but Col. Williams had brought with him, only the day before this action, several officers who would have been unknown to the Georgians. They would have had no reason to doubt Clary.

Hammond's account continues:

"Our troops, encouraged by this disorder, rushed on with more boldness than prudence. The mounted riflemen on both flanks charged into the ranks of the retreating foe, and they fled and re-crossed the river in great disorder" (Hammond).

According to the Draper account, Capt. Inman was killed at this point in the battle. Shelby's account supports this:

"In this pursuit Capt. Inman was killed while pressing the enemy close in his rear—great merit was due to Capt. Inman for the manner in which he brought on the action—and to which the success of the day was greatly to be attributed" (Shelby, 1814).

It is at the time of the retreat of the British that the following incident is reported by Draper:

"Many of the British and Tories were shot down as they were hastening, pell-mell, across the Enoree at the rocky ford. After they were fairly over, one, not yet too weary to evince his bravado, and attract attention for the moment,

turned up his buttocks in derision at the Americans; when one of the Whig officers, probably Brandon or Steen, said to Golding Tinsley: "Can you turn that insolent braggart over?" "I can try," responded Tinsley, who was known to possess a good rifle, when, suiting the action to the word, he took prompt aim, and fired-and sure enough, turned him over, when some of his comrades picked the fellow up, and carried him off" (Draper, 1881:110-111).

Golding Tinsley was a local Patriot who fought at Musgrove's Mill, King's Mountain and Blackstocks. In his pension application he does not mention his participation at Musgrove's Mill although he does relate that much of his service was performed under the command of Col. Williams and he would have been with that militia at the time of the battle. He settled in the area and died at the age of ninety-five. He is buried close to the Musgrove Mill site at the Bobo-Ducker Cemetery at Cross Anchor in Spartanburg County, South Carolina.

Draper published his work in 1881 so the accounts he recorded were collected by correspondence from people who contributed anecdotes passed down in their families or by their neighbors. Although these accounts are anecdotal, they do reflect the richness of the traditions which remained long after the event.

Draper depended heavily on the accounts of John H. Logan who collected his material on the history of the upper country of South Carolina prior to 1859. His first volume was published in that year. Logan had begun collecting material on the Revolutionary War from survivors who lived in the area, planning a second volume. Draper came to South Carolina in 1871 and copied Logan's notes which he incorporated into his own work.

Logan, who knew Golding Tinsley, wrote:

"MUSGROVE"S MILL BATTLE-- Tinsley was also in this fight. He said they killed many British and Tories as they fled across the stream, and shot them while they were in the act of crossing. After they had got over, one fellow squatted down, turned his buttocks and stopped in derision of the Americans. Tinsley's commander said to him "Can't you turn that fellow over?' Tinsley replied, "I can try." Tinsley had a good rifle, sat down, took good aim and turned him over. They took him up and carried him off" (Logan, 1859:391).

Interestingly enough, there is another entry on Golding in the Logan accounts:

"BLACKSTOCK'S BATTLE—I have heard Golding Tinsley talk a great deal about the war. He was at Blackstock's, when Major Money, a British officer, was riding in front on a white horse. Someone of Tinsley's commanders said to him: "Can't you throw that fellow?" Tinsley replied, "I can try." He took aim at him, and he fell to rise no more" (Logan, 1859:351).

Logan continues with: *"Tinsley was at the Cowpens. He was a valiant soldier. He has been dead some 5 or 6 years."*

O'Kelley, in his discussion of the Battle of Blackstock's writes:

"Golding Tinsley was the man who shot Money. Joseph Hart said that Tinsley told him 'Several of the boys had shot at him. At length I told them to give me a crack. He was on an Excellently trained horse, which kept moving backwards and forwards across an opening in the woods in front of us. As he passed this time, I fired, and he fell from his horse.' The grandson of Tinsley was told that Money remained on the battlefield. 'When they went down to where he lay one of them pulled out of his pocket a fine gold watch and presented

it to my father and said he was entitled to it and his reply was he had no use for it'" (O'Kelley, Vol. Two, 2004:557).

The account of the watch is certainly in error as Money did not remain on the field. Lt. Col. Banastre Tarleton rode into the battle and rode off with Money. The heroic act was to no avail as Money died of his wounds.

It is interesting to speculate if the story got embellished with repeating, the older Golding Tinsley got. In any case, it adds to the richness of the narrative.

Hammond continues his account:

"On our part, we were so scattered and out of order, that it was determined to halt, form, and send for our horses to cross the river. This caused a necessary pause, during which we received information, by express, that General Gates had been defeated and his army dispersed; that Colonel Sumter, after much success, had been overtaken by the enemy, and also defeated and his army dispersed; that to crown all, that Colonel Ferguson was advancing towards us, and within a few miles, with a considerable force. Thus circumstanced, we were compelled to give over further pursuit, and seek our own safety by a hasty retreat." (Hammond).

If the dates of the battles are accurate, it is unlikely that Hammond was informed of Sumter's defeat while he was still at Musgrove's Mill. Because of this, Draper dismissed Hammond's account as unreliable. Yet there is little doubt that Hammond was present and active during the battle. By the time he wrote about the battle, he certainly knew that Sumter had been defeated and mistakenly thought the express had contained that information.

Joseph McJunkin makes the same statement in his very brief account of the battle in his pension statement dated 25th day of December 1833:

"I then fell under the Command of Col. Williams & hearing at Smith's ford that the British and Tories were encamped at Musgrove's Mill on the Enoree River marched 40 miles that night and attacked the Tories as day broke and defeated them on 20th August 1780, and at the Close of this action we received Word that both Sumpter & Gates were defeated, which caused us to abandon the idea of Crossing the River to attack the British; having passed Ferguson on our right we retreated towards the mountains." (McJunkin, 1833).

In an 1837 narrative, McJunkin wrote:

"Col. Williams, Col. Streen and myself one of his captains, with those who had a disposition to annoy the British and Tories at Ninety Six, by various marches went up to Smith's Ford on Broad River, & lay one day & one evening of the 18th of August, took up our line of march for Musgrove's Mill. On our march we were overtaken by Francis Jones, who informed us of the defeat of Gen. Gates &Sumter's defeat. Continuing our march, & leaving Col. Ferguson a little to our right, reaching the Tory camp, 300 strong, forty miles from Smith's Ford, at the dawn of day, & commenced the fight; killed a great many, took many prisoners, & marched forty miles to North Tyger. The reason for our rapid march to North Tiger was this: The Tory prisoners told us, that there were 400 British soldiers under the command of Col. Innes, encamped just over the river, and Knowing that Col. Ferguson whom we had just passed a little on our right, must also have heard our firing, & not knowing but that they would break in upon us (who were only about 150 strong), & serve us worse than we did the Tories. We got our water as we passed the brooks, & hunger was so great that we pulled green corn and ate it as we marched" (McJunkin, 1837).

McJunkin's report paints a different picture of the sequence of events and the date is changed from the 20th to the 18th. However, this report was written 57 years after the fact and may not have been written by McJunkin (Graves, 2012: 267-271).

The retreat from the battlefield was hurried as the Americans expected a British patrol to return after hearing the fire.

"This action was one of the hardest ever fought in the United States with small arms. The smoke was so thick as to hide a man at the distance of twenty yards---Our men took two hundred prisoners during the action, and would have improved the victory to great advantage, their object was to be in Ninety Six that night distant 25 or 30 miles and weak and defenseless. But just after the close of the action an express arrived from General McDowell with a letter to him from Governor Caswell informing of the defeat on the 16th of our Grand Army under General Gates near Camden. In this situation to secure a safe retreat was a most difficult task our small party broke down with fatigue two hundred British prisoners in charge, upwards of forty miles advance of General McDowell who retreated immediately and dispersed upon the receipt of the news of Gates's defeat--Ferguson with 3000 men almost directly in their rear. It required all the Vigilance and exertion which human nature was capable of to avoid being cut to pieces by Ferguson's light parties-- it was known to Col. Shelby that he had a body of dragoons and mounted men. That would endeavor to intercept him which caused him to bear up towards the mountains. The enemy pursued as was expected fifty or sixty miles until their horses broke down and could follow no further--It is to be remarked that during the advance of upwards of forty miles and the retreat of fifty or sixty, the Americans never stopped to eat, but made use of peaches and green corn for their support. The excessive fatigue to which they were subjected

for two nights and two days effectually broke down every officer on our side that their faces & eyes swelled and became bloated in appearance as scarcely to be able to see.

"This action happened at the most gloomy period of the revolution just after the defeat and dispersion of the American army, and is not known in the history of the Revolution. After our party had retreated into North Carolina clear of their pursuers, Colonel Shelby crossed the mountains to his own country and left the prisoners taken in the action in the possession of Col. Clarke to carry them on to the North until they could be safely secured; he gave them up shortly after to Colonel John Williams to conduct them to Hillsborough in North Carolina, at this period there was not the appearance of a Corps of Americans embodied anywhere to the Southward of Virginia--In this action the Americans loss was small compared with that of the enemy who over shot them as they lay concealed behind their breast works. The loss of Capt. Inman was much regretted, he fell gloriously fighting for his country on the 19th of August, 1780, with many other brave spirits who volunteered their services on that occasion and defeated the enemy far superior in force to their own" (Shelby, 1814).

Hammond's account is similar although he does not mention the number of prisoners, surely far fewer than Shelby's two hundred.

"The result of this little affair was a clear speck in the horizon, which would have been otherwise very much overcast. We had one captain-S. Inman-a brave man and good officer, with four men killed and eleven men wounded. The British lost Major Fraser, and eighty-five men killed; Captain Innis and several other officers wounded, the number not known. One captain of regulars, two captains of tories, and seventy-three privates--mostly York volunteers-- were taken prisoners. Our retreat was hasty, and continued,

without halting, day or night, to feed or rest, for two days and nights. We entered North-Carolina, and passed down towards Charlotte with our prisoners. Colonel Shelby left us near Greenville, and we encamped near Charlotte, with a few continental troops who had escaped from Gates' defeat. We made a stand here, to collect more men from the defeat, and form for a further expedition. Here the prisoners were committed to Major S. Hammond, while Colonels Williams and Clarke returned to the western frontier of South-Carolina. The prisoners were conducted to Hillsboro' and delivered up there. This little affair, trifling as it may seem, did much good in the general depression of that period. Our numbers continued to increase from that time, and all seemed to have more confidence in themselves" (Hammond).

The British patrol did return shortly after the battle and, seeing the carnage on the battlefield, rode to pursue the Patriots. The patrol was forced to end the pursuit when their horses were too fatigued to continue. It should be noted that this area was considered to have been controlled by Major Ferguson, and is the second time Ferguson was thwarted by backcountry militia under the command of Shelby and Clarke. A determined officer, he would make another attempt that would end at King's Mountain.

There is yet another story connected with the battle. Draper writes the following based on Logan's notes:

"Some interesting incidents connected with, and following the battle, deserve a place in this connection. So many of the British and Tory reserve as could, mounted to the top of Musgrove's house, that they might witness the contest, not doubting for a moment that King George's men could and would bear down all before them. They saw the heroic Inman deliver his successive fires and retreat, followed closely by Innes' pursuers; and supposed this little band constituted the whole of the Rebel party. To these house-top observers, the bold invaders were beaten back-

routed; when they threw up their hats, indulging in shouts that made the old hill in the rear of Musgrove's resound again, and echoes and re-echoes, in commemoration of their imagined victory. At length, reaching the concealed Whigs, a tremendous fire burst upon their pursuers, which caused a deathly paleness on the countenance of some fifty of the reserve party, who were as was said, paroled British prisoners, doing duty contrary to the laws of war-they, especially, dreading the consequences of a possible capture at the hands of the Americans. Their shouting ceased- they peered anxiously, with bated breath, towards the contending parties. At length they raised the cry of despair: "We are beaten-our men are retreating;" and long before the Tories had re-crossed the river, these demoralized Britons had seized their knap-sacks, and were scampering off towards Ninety-Six at their liveliest speed" (Draper, 1881:111-112).

The suggestion that fifty men were crowded on the top of a house seems unrealistic although the house standing at the time Draper wrote was a large house. However, was it the house that stood when the battle occurred? Musgrove family tradition related that the original house was burned by the Tories close to the end of the war in retaliation for Musgrove's Patriot activities. Was the later house built on the same site?

Remains of a burned structure have been found on the site on the top of a hill overlooking the floodplain of the Enoree. Was that the site of the original house? The site is under investigation and, at present, the remains of a foundation and metal objects, showing the evidence of having been burned, only attest to the fact that at some time there was a building on top of the hill which was burned. Was it an early Musgrove dwelling or an outbuilding for the mill?

A descendent of the Musgrove family wrote the following:

"It was by reason of the brave deeds of this girl and of her father in helping the Americans that their home was burned by the Tories and the two were forced to wander homeless to find a resting place with friends" (Childs, 1911:61).

Mrs. Childs, who wrote the account, had preceded this passage with a discussion of Mary Musgrove and her father as they were portrayed in **Horseshoe Robinson** by Kennedy. We can be sure, if the above account is true, it was a large family who had to seek shelter, not merely Mary and her father. However, the family history apparently relates that the original house was burned. Was it rebuilt on the same foundation, or was it elsewhere on the property? That question may be answered with addition research on the hilltop site.

There were lessons to be learned from the battle at Musgrove's Mill and it is interesting to speculate about whether or not those lessons were learned.

The Patriot commanders saw the advantage of massing the militia. They represented North Carolina (now East Tennessee), South Carolina, and Georgia and had fought under a combined command. It was decided before they parted that they would keep in touch and, if one were threatened, they would all respond. They left the field knowing they were capable of inflicting serious damage on British soldiers. They had proved that at Musgrove's Mill.

Had the British learned any lessons from their defeat at Musgrove's Mill? We shall see.

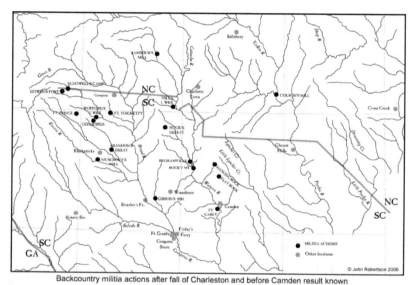

Backcountry militia actions after fall of Charleston and before Camden result known

(Prepared by John Robertson)

Note: Will Graves, webmaster of:

www.southerncampaigns.org/pen

has assembled a list of possible combatants of the Battle of Musgrove's Mill. That information is available on that site as B116. Graves has based his list on his years of researching Patriot commander, Col. James Williams, as well as his work on pension applications.

CHAPTER SEVEN

After Musgrove's Mill

In **South Carolina Loyalists in the American Revolution** Robert Lambert refers to the activities in the backcountry as *"a number of small-scale engagements...rarely more than skirmishes"* (Lambert, 1987:133). He continues:

> *"These actions were climaxed by the truly significant battle at Musgrove's Mill near the Enoree River; in this action, Alexander Innes led part of his South Carolina Royalists, just returned from furlough or recently recruited, and Daniel Clary's militia in an attack on a party of rebels, but they were repulsed with heavy loss, Innes himself suffering a serious wound in the neck. The triumphant rebels were planning to follow their victory by mounting an assault against the base at Ninety-Six, but they beat a hasty retreat when they received word of Gate's defeat. Following Camden and Tarleton's rout of Sumter, the northwestern part of the province was returned to British and loyalist control for the time being"* (Lambert, 1987:133).

It is difficult to reconcile the idea of the northwestern part of the province as being under British and Loyalist control in light of the Patriot activities previously discussed. From Huck's Defeat on 12 July the British and Tories had been under constant attack in the backcountry. The British had lost Gowen's Old Fort, Fort Prince and Fort Anderson (Fort

Thicketty). They had been pushed out of the campsite at Musgrove's Mill and would make no effort to reestablish it. Further, the Provincial prisoners taken in the running battle through Wofford's Iron Works and Lawson's Fork had been transported over the mountains to what is now Eastern Tennessee. The prisoners taken at Musgrove's Mill were now interned at Hillsborough, North Carolina, guarded by the Southern Continental Army.

Although the Patriot militia had rapidly moved north and west after the action at Musgrove's Mill, they were not idle. When Elijah Clarke returned to Georgia, he immediately planned an attack on Augusta. The British post at Augusta threatened the security of Wilkes County, the home of most of Clarke's militia.

In June, 1780, at about the same time British soldiers occupied Ninety-Six, Lt. Col. Thomas Brown led his King's Rangers into Augusta. In 1775 Brown had been tarred and feathered in this area and the cruel treatment had burned off two of his toes: thus the name, Burnfoot Brown. Brown had previously been in South Carolina.

"Because of Burnfoot Brown's habit of using torture, Cornwallis ordered him out of South Carolina and into Georgia, where he continued his old ways" (Edgar, 2001:131).

Now, back at the scene of his humiliation, he was determined to wipe out any resistance by hanging anyone he perceived as a threat to his authority.

To strengthen his control of the area, Brown courted the disaffected Indians in the area who had been alienated by Whig control after the earlier withdrawal of the British from Augusta on 13 February 1779. One of his methods was to provide provisions to the Indians. Those provisions were stored at Augusta and Clarke hoped to seize them.

It was difficult to recruit Patriot militia after the disastrous defeat of the Continentals at Camden but, through threats and appeals, Clarke was able to muster a number of Wilkes County militia. He appealed for help from South Carolina and Major James McCall, who had accompanied Andrew Pickens into Georgia and fought at the Battle of Kettle Creek (Swager, 2008) and had joined Clarke at Musgrove's Mill, arrived with a much smaller complement than expected. McCall had begged Andrew Pickens to join the expedition but Pickens had taken a parole and would honor it until a violation persuaded him otherwise (Rauch, 2005).

It is not the purpose of this text to cover the details of the engagement which are meticulously described in Steven Rauch's article. This siege lasted 4 days and Clarke appeared to have been successful. However, relief for Brown's surrounded post came when troops from Ninety-Six, under the command of Lt. Col. John Cruger, arrived and, in the resulting action, about 60 of Clarke's men were killed or wounded.

Retribution was swift in coming and thirteen Patriots were hanged at Brown's headquarters. Lt. Col. Cruger:

"..sent detachments in all directions to mete out frontier justice to the guerillas, their families and any others who demonstrate sympathy for the Whig cause" (Rauch, 2005:13).

The Wilkes Country courthouse and frontier forts which provided protection against Indian attacks were burned as well as over 100 homes. Col. John Dooley, who had taken British protection under the provisions of parole, was murdered by Tories. The brutality of the British tactics in Wilkes County was probably unequaled in the entire conflict.

Toward the end of September, Clarke mustered his militia at Petersburg, a settlement on the Savannah River, north of Augusta. Three hundred men arrived with four hundred women and children. They had rations for about five days. There was no safety in Georgia and Clarke realized that the only sanctuary for his beleaguered people would be over the mountains to the north.

He began a march of over two hundred miles through trackless mountain terrain. His destination was the area which is now Eastern Tennessee. The valleys of the Nolichucky and Watauga Rivers were home to militia commanders Col. John Sevier and Col. Isaac Shelby and to their men. The British had never been able to breach the mountains and, if the Georgians could get over the mountains, they would be safe.

When Lt. Col. Cruger reported the exodus to Lord Cornwallis, Major Patrick Ferguson was dispatched from the Charlotte area with orders to intercept Clarke. It surely was not lost on the British that the combined militia units of Shelby and Clarke had inflicted considerable damage on the British Provincials under Ferguson's command and were still holding some of his Provincials as prisoners in the Watauga area.

The exact route Clarke took is unknown although the pension application of David Thurmond (available on southerncampaigns.org/pen) gives the most complete account available. According to that account, the Georgians crossed the Savannah River where it joined the Tugaloo. They stopped at Green River at a place called Price's Settlement, a place unknown today. It was the only stop where food was available on the entire trip.

From the diary of Allaire who rode with Ferguson, we do know where Clarke was not traveling. He was not on the road. It is assumed that the Georgians followed Indian trails along the base of the Appalachian Mountains. However, when an exasperated Ferguson failed to find Clarke, he sent an ultimatum across the mountains to Shelby. He threatened that if Shelby and his followers did not return their prisoners, turn in their weapons and pledge allegiance to the King, Ferguson would go to their settlements, hang them and lay waste their homes with fire and sword.

The thought that such a threat would not intimidate the Over Mountain Men, but embolden them, was lost on the British. John Buchanan writes as follows:

"The Over Mountain Man, hardened by the toil of pioneering, was further hardened by Indian fighting. His life could indeed be short, nasty, and brutal. But if he survived falling trees, fever, snakes bites, drowning, disease, backbreaking labor, blood poisoning, and the scalping knife, he rode into a fight a warrior for the ages" (Buchanan, 1997:207).

Col. Shelby did what was planned after Musgrove's Mill. He would call out an army of militia and confront and destroy Ferguson. He first rode to the Nolichucky settlement to meet with Col. John Sevier, the commander of the Washington County militia. Sevier agreed with Shelby's plan and pledged to support the campaign. The word was spread to assemble at Sycamore Shoals on 25 September. They had no commissary and no source of supply. At the appointed time so many assembled that some had to be turned back to protect the communities from Indian attack while the bulk of the militia traveled across the mountains to confront Ferguson.

"Each had a rolled blanket in which to sleep, a cup with which to drink, and a wallet or saddle bags filled with food, mainly parched corn meal mixed with maple sugar that could be eaten cold or warmed up with a bit of water. The horses were expected to find their own forage when hobbled during stops and at night. The Over Mountain Men were armed with tomahawks, and large knives for cutting, eating, fighting and scalping. Across the pommels of their saddles rested their principal weapon, for which they were famous on two continents - the American rifle" (Buchanan, 1997:213).

As the Over Mountain men crossed the mountains and moved towards South Carolina, they were joined by militia from Virginia, North Carolina and South Carolina. Col. James Williams arrived with his Little River militia as he had promised. But where were Col. Clarke and his Georgians? They, too, had promised to support Shelby.

According to the very limited amount of information about Clarke's exodus from Georgia, it appears he was lost. The landmarks mentioned suggest he was between Mount Mitchell and Mount Pisgah. That would put him in the vicinity of present-day Asheville, North Carolina. Now the Georgians were confronted with the Smokey Mountains and had no guide to lead them across.

As fortune or Providence would have it, a group of militia moving from the Holson River area of Virginia had crossed the Smokies and found the exhausted and half-starved Georgians. From the commander, Capt. Edward Hampton, the Georgians learned about Ferguson's threat. Elijah Clarke must have been conflicted. He had promised to respond but he had the welfare of four hundred women and children to consider.

Elijah Clarke would detach about thirty of his militia under the command of Major William Candler and Capt. Stephen Johnson to accompany the Virginians. Clarke would lead the rest of the Georgians through Sam's Gap which Hampton's men had told him about. Clarke had been wounded at Wofford's Iron Works, at Musgrove's Mill and at Augusta, and that may have affected his decision not to accompany his men to join Shelby. In any case, the thirty Georgians would join Shelby's army of militia and be attached to Col. Williams's command in the approaching battle.

On 7 October the combined forces of militia from Virginia, North Carolina, South Carolina and Georgia surrounded Major Ferguson's force at King's Mountain. In the hard-fought battle, Ferguson was killed and his forces killed, wounded or taken prisoner. The Patriot casualties included Col. James Williams who was fatally shot in the final stages of the battle.

The details of Williams' death are conflicting. Hill, who disliked Williams intensely, suggested that Williams had been shot by his own men, a charge which is totally without support. An interesting account is related in Logan.

"Williams and Ferguson fell nearly at the same time, on the Eastern end of the mountain. Williams from a more elevated and favorable position than those occupied by Campbell or Hambright, saw the magic influence of Ferguson's whistle. Dashing to the front, his horse throwing bloody foam from his mouth that had been struck by a ball, he was heard to exclaim : 'I'll silence that whistle, or die in the attempt.' Quickly Ferguson was no more, and soon from a ball from the enemy laid Williams mortally wounded on the hillside" (Logan, 1859:412).

Logan had interviewed many men who had fought at King's Mountain and had walked the battle field with his grandfather who had fought there.

A primary source from Alexander Chesney, a Loyalist who accompanied Ferguson to King's Mountain, relates this event:

"Col. Ferguson was at last recognized by his gallantry although wearing a hunting shirt and fell pierced by seven balls at the moment he had killed the American Col. Williams with his left hand; (the right hand being useless) I had just rallied the troops a second time by Ferguson's orders when Cap DePeyster succeeded to the command but soon gave up and sent out a flag of truce" (Moss, 2002:32).

Moss reports in a footnote that *"The claim that Ferguson killed Col. Williams is verified by at least one other loyalist"* (Moss, 2002:32).

While we will never know how it happened, it is interesting to speculate if it could have happened as Chesney relates. Could Major Patrick Ferguson, who lost the use of his right arm after the battle of Brandywine, have used his left hand to shoot Williams? That seems highly unlikely.

It will probably never be known how Williams died but a teenage boy who rode with the Little River Militia, Thomas Young, reported that Williams was wounded at the end of the battle. Young ran to him and reports that the last words Williams spoke were: *"For God's sake, boys, don't give up the hill,"* which suggests that the Patriots were in control of the mountain when Williams was shot (Young, in Meltzer, 1987:150). Whatever occurred on that mountain, Col. James Williams was the highest ranking officer killed in the battle.

In the years immediately after the battle, the references to Williams were highly complementary. However, after Draper published Hill's vitriolic account which Hill's family reported was dictated "in his dotage," Williams' reputation was damaged.

In his latest book on James Williams, Will Graves concludes:

"What Williams' Tory enemies could not do, Hill did with his accusations. Williams' dogged commitment to the Patriot cause entitles him to a better legacy than that fashioned for him by Hill. While Williams' role as one of the nine commanders of the Patriot militia forces at the battle does not entitle him to be known as 'the Hero of King's Mountain,' he is entitled to be included, without caveat or reservation, among the many heroes who selflessly served his country in its fight for independence. Indeed, his legacy should rate him among the pantheon of South Carolina's Revolutionary era military heroes, men such as Francis Marion, Thomas Sumter, Andrew Pickens, John Laurens, William Henderson and William Moultrie" (Graves, 2012: 172).

If the British thought they had control of the countryside after Musgrove's Mill, it was only seven weeks before the reality of their situation was evidenced. Lord Cornwallis saw that his western flank was vulnerable to the attack of well-trained and fearless militiamen and he moved his headquarters from Charlotte, North Carolina, back to Winnsboro, South Carolina. General Clinton, the British commander in the colonies, would later comment:

"an event which was immediately productive of the worst consequences to the King's affairs in South Carolina, and unhappily proved the first link in a chain of evils that followed each other in regular succession until they at last ended in a total loss of America" (Clinton: 1954:226).

CHAPTER EIGHT

More Trouble in the Back Country

If the British had not learned the threat of this back country militia at Musgrove's Mill, it appears they had not learned from King's Mountain.

In November, Col. Thomas Sumter moved into the area south of the Tyger River. He was accompanied by Elijah Clarke and Wilkes County militia and Major James McCall's South Carolina Dragoons who had fought at Musgrove's Mill, as well as other militia from Burke County, Georgia. Fearing an attack on the British post at Ninety-Six, Lord Cornwallis sent Lt. Col. Banastre Tarleton to confront Sumter.

Tarleton was the most successful of the British officers in the Carolinas but was the most hated by the Patriots. He had allowed his troopers to cut down prisoners at Monck's Corner and at the Waxhaws and was known as 'Bloody Tarleton.' At the Battle of Camden, when the Patriot militia fled, Tarleton's troops pursued the desperate men, cutting them down as they ran. He had the utmost contempt for the colonists in general, and the Patriot militia in particular. Now he would pursue Sumter's combined militia force.

In addition to his British Legion, Tarleton commanded the 63rd Regiment of Foot, and a battalion of the 71st Regiment of Foot, Fraser's Highlanders, and artillery. However, wanting to attack Sumter before the Patriots could get back across the Tyger River, Tarleton left his infantry and artillery behind and rushed toward Sumter's position at Blackstock's farm. In the attack, militia riflemen, shooting from the protection of buildings and behind fences, drove back the British. O'Kelley reports:

"The British rallied their exhausted men and retreated in order, but they left the field with half of their men lost to the action" (O'Kelley, 2004: Vol. 2, 371).

The Patriots suffered three killed and four wounded. Col. Thomas Sumter was severely wounded and carried from the battlefield. As night approached, the Patriots built fires to suggest to any spies that they were camped for the night. Under cover of darkness the Patriots crossed the Tyger River and departed the area.

The following day, Tarleton arrived on the scene with his entire command, expecting to engage Sumter's force again. His quarry had fled and he had only to bury his dead. However, since the empty field was now his, he proclaimed the engagement a victory:

"Three of the enemy's colonels fell in the action, and General Sumpter received a severe wound in the shoulder. Upwards of one hundred Americans were killed and wounded, and fifty were made prisoners. On the side of the British, Lieutenants Gibson and Cope of the 63rd were killed; and Lieutenant Money, aid-de-camp to Earl Cornwallis, who had commanded the detachment of mounted infantry, with great gallantry, was mortally wounded; Another officer of the 63rd, and two subalterns of the British legion, were likewise wounded. The former corps had also thirty, and the latter fifteen, non-commissioned officers and men, with thirty horses, killed and wounded (Tarleton, 1787:179-180).

The difference between the American reports of the battle and Tarleton's account might have remained unsettled but for the account of Roderick MacKenzie, an officer in the 71st Regiment of Foot. After the publication of Tarleton's history of his campaigns, MacKenzie wrote a rebuttal:

"The real truth is, that the Americans being well sheltered, sustained very inconsiderable loss in the attack: and, as for the three Colonels, they must certainly have been imaginary beings, "Men in buckram," created merely to grace the triumph of a victory, which the British army in Carolina were led to celebrate, amidst the contempt and derision of the inhabitants, who had much better information" (MacKenzie, 1787:77-78).

Again, the British had underestimated the courage and resolve of the militia. The success of the militia at Musgrove's Mill, King's Mountain, and Blackstock's would continue to impact the events in the backcountry.

However, there was trouble ahead for the Patriots. On 12 December 1780, a British force from Ninety-Six attacked Elijah Clarke's camp at Cane Creek and overwhelmed the Georgia militia and James McCall's dragoons. Eight Georgians were killed and Elijah Clarke and James McCall were both wounded. Clarke was carried from the field with what appeared to be a chest wound and the British were convinced that it was a mortal wound and they had killed Clarke. The British withdrew leaving a detachment under the command of Capt. James Dunlap to complete the operation. Dunlap soon learned that Clarke had not been killed but was seriously wounded. Dunlap was determined to hunt down his adversary.

Dunlap's men first went to the home of James McCall and, finding neither of the men they sought, they plundered the home, abused the family and left Mrs. McCall and her children destitute in the cold December weather. That brutality would be remembered!

Next, Captain Dunlap's behavior initiated a series of events which surely impacted on the outcome of the war in the back country. He violated Andrew Pickens's parole.

Col. Andrew Pickens was well-known and respected by the settlers in the backcountry of the Carolinas and Georgia. He had a long history as an Indian fighter, and had earlier been a serious threat to the British in Georgia. Pickens and his good friend, James McCall, had joined with Georgia's Wilkes County militia in February of 1779 to defeat the Loyalist commander, Col. Boyd, at Kettle Creek (Swager, 2008). He was acquainted with Elijah Clarke and the two had campaigned together.

However, Pickens had taken a parole and had honored that parole even when his friend, James McCall, had urged him to return to the fight. The British had treated Pickens well, hoping to have him pledge allegiance to the King. He had been offered money, land, and a commission in the British army but he had refused and remained neutral. Believing that Clarke could have found sanctuary with his old friend, Dunlap attacked Pickens's plantation. Andrew Pickens was absent when Dunlap's troops destroyed property and threatened the Pickens family.

When Pickens returned he was outraged and announced to the British that he had kept his word and honored his parole but the British had not. Andrew Pickens would return to the fight even with a 'halter round his neck.' In other words, if the British should capture Pickens in arms, he would be hanged without trial.

The incident could not have been more fortunate for the Patriots. The Continental Army in the South had a new commander, Major General Nathanael Greene. He had sent the most capable of his army under the command of Brigadier General Daniel Morgan into the area along the North and South Carolina border with orders to 'annoy the enemy and spirit up the people.' The people Greene wanted 'spirited up' were the militia. He had learned of the militia victory at King's Mountain and Blackstock's as he traveled south, and realized their value. Although he would have preferred to fight the British with only his Continentals, he realized that his army was undermanned and poorly armed. He needed militia.

Greene expected Thomas Sumter's militia would support Morgan, but the wounded Sumter refused to allow his officers to take orders from any but himself and he refused to support Morgan. Now Morgan was camped at Grindal Shoals on the west side of the Pacolet River with only local militia support guarding the eastern side of the Pacolet River.

On Christmas Day, Col. Andrew Pickens arrived at Morgan's camp, accompanied by about 100 men including some of his old Long Cane militia, and his friend, Major James McCall and his South Carolina Dragoons. He offered his service to Morgan and that service was enthusiastically accepted. Col. Andrew Pickens would call out the backcountry militia to support Morgan. Would they respond?

Col. Thomas Sumter was a popular and powerful commander, and the pious Pickens lacked that charisma. It was reported that Pickens rarely spoke and never smiled. He was an elder in the Presbyterian Church and was called the Fighting Elder. However, he had earned the respect of the people in this area. He was feared by the Indians and revered by the settlers. He left Morgan's camp to muster the militia.

Major James McCall and his men remained with Morgan and were attached to Lt. Col. William Washington's Virginia Cavalry. McCall's men became the eyes and ears of the Virginians as these locals knew every settler, river, ford and road.

On 30 December, at Hammond's Store, Washington and McCall attacked a Tory force commanded by Georgia Loyalist Col. Thomas Waters. The Tories were moving east to join Lord Cornwallis. Thomas Young, a militiaman, reported the event:

"When we came in sight, we perceived that the Tories had formed in a line on the brow of the hill opposite to us. We had a long hill to descend and another to rise. Col. Washington and his dragoons gave a shout, drew swords, and charged down the hill like madmen. The Tories fled in every direction without firing a gun. We took a great many prisoners and killed a few" (Thomas Young, 1843).

O'Kelley reports that the casualties were 150 killed and wounded and 40 captured Loyalists. The Americans suffered no casualties (O'Kelley, 2004: Vol. 2:394)!

Lt. Col. William Washington and Major James McCall then moved to Fort Williams, the plantation home of the deceased Col. James Williams. The property had been established as Ferguson's headquarters earlier and had been named Fort Williams. The Tories manning the fort fled at the approach of the Patriot cavalry and the fort was taken. This site was about fifteen miles from the British outpost at Ninety-Six and Lord Cornwallis, camped at Winnsboro, had to respond. He had watched and waited and now, fearing Morgan would move against Ninety-Six, he sent Lt. Col. Banastre Tarleton into the field to destroy Morgan.

Robert Stokesbury writes:

"For ten days in early January Tarleton first looked for and then chased Morgan, whom he outnumbered two to one. On January 17 he made the mistake of catching him.

"Morgan was a canny old dog, and he took up a position in rolling, more or less open, country, on a rise of ground known as The Cowpens. He put his little army in three lines, a screen of riflemen out front, then the South Carolina militia, and finally his Continentals and some more Virginia riflemen in the main line, keeping his light dragoons in reserve. He told everybody what he wanted: from the first two lines, two good hits, not just shots but hits, then file off and reform behind the main line. This was just about what

militia usually could do anyway, and seldom has a battle plan been better suited to the material at hand" (Stokesbury, 1991:237).

Brigadier General Daniel Morgan, a rifleman himself, had inflicted heavy damage on Burgoyne's British troops at Saratoga. He knew that the time required to reload would leave the militia vulnerable to a bayonet attack. He depended on them to take out British officers and sergeants with accurate fire, then withdraw and regroup. These were the men Tarleton despised. He believed they would not stand and fight. Had the British learned anything from Musgrove's Mill, King's Mountain, and Blackstock's? Apparently not!

"Tarleton came on like the young dandy he was, a fine commander grown careless from poor opposition" (Stokesbury, 1991:237).

Skirmishers met Tarleton's light infantry with rifle fire and the mounted British retreated. This prevented Tarleton from learning the surprises Morgan had in store for him. Tarleton pressed on and his troops moved toward the now assembled militia line. Would they not flee in the face of British bayonets?

The militia line stood and waited as the British troops advanced towards them in a sort of trot. Militia officers ordered the militia to hold their fire until the order was given. Suddenly, the militia line fired into the approaching British with deadly effect. They then moved back through the Continental line in an *en echelon* movement, to reform. They had done as Morgan asked. They had targeted the officers and sergeants and it had worked.

Roderick McKenzie, an officer in the 71st Regiment of Foot, the Frazer's Highlanders, surveyed the damage. When his unit, held in reserve, attacked the Continentals, he reported:

"A number, not less than two-thirds of the British infantry officers, had already fallen, and nearly the same proportion of privates" (McKenzie, 1787:91).

Morgan lured the British into a series of killing zones and in less than an hour it was over (Babits, 1998).

"In an hour's work he (Tarleton) had lost more than 900 men, of whom a hundred were killed and the rest wounded or captured or both.....and the American cause in the Carolinas was once again alive and well" (Stokesbury, 1991:237).

With no place to secure the prisoners he had taken, Morgan quickly moved his army to the north on a long journey across North Carolina to Virginia. He was accompanied by Andrew Pickens and part of the militia which had performed so gallantly at the battle. They were joined by the remainder of the army under the command of General Nathanael Greene.

Lord Cornwallis and the defeated Tarleton pursued the Continentals and their accompanying militia but failed to recover the British prisoners. Now, at least part of the British army was gone from the Carolinas. Five months after his splendid victory over the Continental Army in Camden, Lord Cornwallis left this area to his commanders in Camden, Ninety-Six and Charleston. He would never return.

The disastrous defeats of the Americans at Charleston and Camden had not resulted in victory for the British army. In the darkest days of the war, the militia had taken the field and, in a series of encounters, had inflicted serious casualties on the British Provincials and Regulars.

Walter Edgar identifies Huck's Defeat in what is now York County as:

"the first of thirty-five battles in which the state's freedom fighters challenged the army of occupation and its Tory Allies....during the five-and-a-half months period. The

partisans lost 497 killed or wounded and 320 prisoners of war. The British and Tory casualties were 1,200 killed or wounded and 1,286 prisoners of war" (Edgar, 2001:143).

"Each of these engagements played a major role in leading up to the decisive battle at King's Mountain. Without the partisan victories at Huck's Defeat, Stallions, Cedar Springs, Gowen's Old Fort, Thicketty Fort, Hanging Rock and Musgrove's Mill, there would have been no battle at King's Mountain. Had these engagements-and other nameless skirmishes- not taken place, Cornwallis would have been able to march unchallenged into North Carolina" (Edgar, 2001:144).

After in-depth research of the conditions and personnel involved in the early militia victory at Huck's Defeat, historian Michael Scoggins wrote:

"In conclusion, the evidence of Huck's defeat and dozens of other battles and skirmishes in the Backcountry clearly demonstrates the effectiveness of the Whig militia in the Carolinas. Operating on their own with little support from the Continental Congress or state governments, forced to provide their own weapons, food and clothing, the militiamen kept up the fight and refused to surrender until the final battle was won. In spite of what many modern historians have claimed, the Backcountry militiamen of the Carolinas and Georgia were a courageous, highly effective, highly motivated military force, and when led by their own officers and allowed to fight on their own terms, they were capable of meeting and defeating larger, better-equipped forces of the British Army on almost every occasion. They successfully waged a partisan war against the most powerful army on earth, and in the process, they not only helped win their country's independence, but they also helped push warfare out of the eighteenth century and into the modern age" (Scoggins, 2005:159).

The men who fought at Musgrove's Mill were among those militiamen who had fought the British and won. What had happened there after that battle?

CHAPTER NINE

Life on the Enoree After the Battle

We have seen that the action after the battle at Musgrove's Mill had moved north. What changes had occurred at the battle site in the Enoree River area as a result?

The Musgrove's Mill site was on the Enoree River crossing for the trail that branched off the main Cherokee Trail. The main trail from Charleston to Fort Loudon in what is now in Tennessee had followed the Saluda River west. Travelers headed for the Pacolet River and the mountains followed a trail which continued along the west side of the Broad River and crossed the Enoree River at Musgrove's. Many militia headed for the new skirmishes and battle sites would have followed this trail.

Did travelers crossing at Musgrove's Mill pause to reflect on the battle which had recently been fought there? Possibly militia who had been there might have related their contributions to the victory. However, there were no monuments or markers other than the tree under which Shadrick Inman rested. Vegetation would have claimed the bloody field and left little evidence of the mass graves in the open ground, or the breastworks along the ridge of the road.

Although the action had moved on, the settlers along the Enoree had been involved in those later battles. Pension applications indicate that many of the same men who fought at Musgrove's Mill also fought at King's Mountain, Blackstock's and/or Cowpens. Major Patrick Ferguson and the Provincials who accompanied him were posted at Ninety-Six and moved north across the Enoree. It was a troublesome time for the Patriots who lived in his path. Militia moving to join in the hunt for Ferguson which ended at King's Mountain travelled along and across the Enoree.

Certainly, when Col. Thomas Sumter moved south of the Tyger River there was considerable activity in the Enoree area. Col. Banastre Tarleton moved into the area to attack Sumter at Blackstock's. Tarleton's own account relates that he moved along the Enoree River (Tarteton, 1787).

Later, as Brigadier General Morgan moved south to the Pacolet, activity increased along the Enoree. As Lt. Col. Banastre Tarleton left Winnsboro, he crossed the Broad River, then crossed the Enoree River at Musgrove Ford as he moved upstream to the west, then turned north to cross the Tyger and the Pacolet (Landrum, 1897).

The Little River Militia, commanded by Col. Joseph Hayes after the death of Col. James Williams at King's Mountain, lived south of the Enoree and many would have used the road across the ford at Musgrove's Mill. Surely the settlers in the area were uneasy. Those who were not involved in the battles were still not safe from enemies passing through their properties.

After the battle at Cowpens, the British forces under Lord Cornwallis left the area to pursue the Continental Army across North Carolina, but there were still British troops at Ninety-Six. Also, Tories who were enraged at the loss at Cowpens attacked neighbors who were Patriots and there are accounts of men surviving the battle only to be slain by neighbors. Such is the nature of internecine war.

The winter of 1780-81 was bitterly cold and wet. Settlers whose homes had been stripped of all household goods struggled to survive. Pension applications reflect the hardships. William Wilbanks fought at Musgrove's Mill. After his death his widow applied for a pension. She reported:

"...that he was absent for a long time, she thinks five years, but certainly not less than four years, off & on, she made three crops without him; herself and her little Boys; and had much trouble with the Tories during the absences of her husband, and labored hard to make a support—the Tories threw down her fences often and she had to put them up herself with her little Boys who were very young & small to do such labor, they also killed her Hogs & Cattle and destroyed everything about the place, very often passing and committing all kinds of depredations all of which she had to suffer with her children unprotected" (William Wilbanks, R11508, widow).

Other pension applications document the losses. John Jenkins wrote:

"That during the war his home was plundered by the enemy took from him five head of horses his cattle his hogs &left him impoverished" (John Jenkins, S31776*).*

Spring of 1781 brought the misery of a smallpox epidemic to the back country. Since militia had not been inoculated as had Continental soldiers, those men suffered severely. Smallpox took the life of Major James McCall, a veteran of Kettle Creek, Musgrove's Mill and the commander of the Patriot mounted militia at Cowpens. Others, who did not die of the disease, were incapacitated for several weeks as the illness ran its course.

Early May brought increased activity along the Enoree as militia moved south to support the Continental Army commanded by Major General Nathanael Greene. Greene moved to siege the British post at Ninety-Six. Again, pension applications of militia relate that they had crossed the Enoree River at Musgrove's ford. Supply wagons for the army rumbled down the road from the north as the siege continued. However, it was all in vain and British reinforcements from Charleston forced Greene to withdraw.

The Continental Army moved north across the Enoree before crossing the Broad River, then heading east to camp for the summer beyond the Wateree River.

After a long winter and a rainy spring, summer was hot and humid with rivers flooded and swamps alive with biting insects. As Greene attempted to assemble a larger army, disease was an additional enemy. Smallpox again plagued the militia. Finally, on 8 September 1781, after a long and bloody battle at Eutaw Springs, the British were forced to retreat to Charleston Neck. It would be the last large battle in the South.

Five weeks after Eutaw Springs, Lord Cornwallis surrendered his army at Yorktown, 19 October 1781.

Surely the citizens of the Carolinas and Georgia must have hoped the warfare was over but it was not to be. Tory leader David Fanning, who had fought for the British at Musgrove's Mill, was raiding Whig neighbors in North Carolina.

In South Carolina, Col. William Cunningham, known as "Bloody Bill" moved into the Ninety-Six district and moved through with murderous intent. With the British gone from Ninety-Six, Cunningham had assembled a large enough force to attack his Patriot neighbors. Starting his rampage along the Saluda he moved to the Hayes Station where he murdered Col. Hayes who had assumed the command of the Little River Militia after Col. James Williams had been killed at King's Mountain. Cunningham also killed the two young sons of Col. Williams who had stayed with the militia.

Patriot militia assembled and tracked Cunningham and surprised him at his encampment. Cunningham escaped on a fast horse to Charleston and was later evacuated to the West Indies when the British left South Carolina.

There was no peace as long as the British maintained a presence in South Carolina, just uneasy watchfulness. Finally, on 14 December 1782, the British and many of their

Tory supporters with families, possessions and slaves, embarked at Charleston. The British were gone.

On 4 February 1783 the British government announced the end of hostilities against the colonies and in March the new nation of the United States of America declared the end of hostilities. The Second Treaty of Paris was signed 3 September 1783.

The war was over!

There were no parades for the militia. No monuments were raised to their contributions on fields of battle. The venues of their bravery remained unmarked and soon were covered with vegetation which grew abundantly in the back country.

Now the task of the settlers was to rebuild their devastated properties and lives. That would be a formidable undertaking. A traveler in the Ninety-Six District after the war reported that there were twelve hundred widows in that district which encompassed the land north of the Saluda River and west of the Broad River. The Ninety-Six District area included, of course, the Enoree River settlers. Even when men had returned from the war, many had wounds that made the hard labor required to rebuild difficult if not impossible.

Pensions had been available for servicemen long before the Revolutionary War as a means of maintaining an army. Now, in 1776, the first pension legislation for the American colonies was enacted. It provided half-pay for officers and enlisted men, including those who served on warships, and for those who were disabled and not able to earn a living. Subsequent legislation extended pensions but still only for officers and enlisted men. However, the settlers who had fought in the battles in the back country of South Carolina had been militia and they were not covered in the early legislation.

Farmers, whose properties had been vandalized, needed seeds, livestock, farm implements, fencing, and almost every necessity of life. Most had no means of purchasing what was needed.

During the war officers gave receipts to citizens who provided supplies or militia service to the Patriot forces. South Carolina promptly addressed these debts and on 22 March 1783 began to issue interest-bearing certificates called indents. The stubs to these certificates were kept by the government and audited accounts and indent stubs are available for researchers at the South Carolina Department of Archives and History in Columbia, South Carolina.

Recipients of these certificates often used them to pay debts accrued as they attempted to rebuild. Others were forced to sell them at a discount to acquire funds. For example, the pension application of Jeremiah Dial, (W914), who served under Capt. Levi Casey in Col. Williams's Regiment,

"he received a certificate of his service which he presented to the Auditor of Charleston sometimes afterwards from whom he received an Indented Certificate of the pay due him for his services—This certificate he bartered away for little or nothing."

There was an effort to provide reimbursement for the service and supplies, but the greatest devastation had been caused by the British troops and their Loyalist adherents. Fences were broken, stock was stolen or slaughtered, homes were burned, crops were destroyed and every sort of abuse was meted out to make the Patriot settlers destitute. There are accounts of even clothing and bedding taken. One woman reported that Tories had taken her mother's wedding ring and the buckles from her shoes. There was no compensation for the losses inflicted by these acts of destruction and vandalism.

Settlers who had some income survived. A miller, such as Edward Musgrove, earned a tenth of everything he milled so he would have grain to sell or barter. However, after

Musgrove died in the 1790s, his wife remarried and, either through mismanagement or the economics of the time, lost the mill and property to George Gordon. The property became Gordon's Mill and is so named in subsequent maps.

Some people not only survived the war but thrived in business and land speculation. However, the farmers who had lost everything found it difficult to start again.

Such misery was not confined to the backcountry of South Carolina and Congress saw the nation's need as years passed to provide some sort of relief for impoverished veterans.

However, it was not until 2 June 1832, (4 Stat. 529) that militia was included and then only those who had served two years would be eligible for a pension for life. Those serving less than two years but for more than six months could receive pensions of less than full pay. Further legislation in 1836 allowed widows of veterans who had performed service to apply for pension.

The pension acts required the veteran or his widow to appear before a court of record to describe, under oath, the service for which the pension was claimed. It is these pension applications, now becoming available to the researcher as well as interested readers, which provide much information on what had happened in these battles and how the participants regarded their service.

Historians may have paid little attention to the militia battles in the back country, but those who fought there remembered those engagements and, fifty years after the battle, they wrote of Musgrove's Mill.

CHAPTER TEN

Voices from Musgrove's Mill

More than fifty years after the war, these survivors, now in their late sixties or older, wrote of the battle at Musgrove's Mill. At those ages memories dim, but for these veterans, what had happened there was an important part of their service. The following comments are extracted from the pension applications available on:

www.southerncampaigns.org/pen

Joseph Alexander (S15355)
I was then attached to the Command under Col. Williams aforesaid. Was then marched to Kings Mountain where we had an engagement against Col. Ferguson of the British Army where said Ferguson was Defeated & killed this as near as I recollect was on 7th Oct. 1780. In Aug. of the same year we had an engagement at Musgrove's Mill in the District then called 96 in South Carolina—

Matthew Alexander (W324)
.. we were marched to Musgrove's Mill on the Enoree River South Carolina where we had a battle with the British and Tories, we took Sixty prisoners or more and got them away with us.

Bailey Anderson (S30826)

The head commander was General McDowell, but there were many other officers in the command. He recollects Colonel Clark of Georgia, Col. Shelby of Holston River, Colonel Williams of South Carolina and his captain's name was Parsons at this time. He marched from the frontier or line of North Carolina to Musgrove's Mill on what was called Enoree River in South Carolina District Ninety Six. About a mile from said Musgrove's Mill [we] fell in with a party of British and Tories and had a fight which was called the Battle of Musgrove's Mill. The Americans defeated the British. But at the finish of the action an express came with information that Generals Gates and Sumpter had been defeated and the detachment to which he belonged retreated as fast as possible to the North Carolina line.

William Black (W9730)

He was afterwards in the Battle of Musgrove's Mill. Here Col. Innis commanded the enemy & Cols. Clarke & Shelby the Americans where we were victorious. There he (William Black) was wounded in the hand by a rifle ball which wound is now plainly to be seen.

Christopher Brandon (S9288)

In the month of May or June 1780, in my sixteenth year under Captain Jolly in Col. Brandon's Regiment in now York District, the day after what was called Brandon's defeat, and thence marched into Rowan County, No. Carolina where I remained until a short time before the battle of Musgrove's on Enoree, Union District,

Ralph Cassel (R1791)

That he entered the service of the United States under the following named Officers & served as herein stated – that he entered the service in the County of Newberry in the State of North Carolina [sic, South Carolina] in the Company commanded by Captain Joseph Hayes, some time in the summer or spring the year 1776 in the Regiment commanded by Colonel Williams [James Williams], that he marched from thence to Musgrove's Mill, on Enoree River and was in an engagement there, that he received a wound in said engagement on his shoulder that they drove the enemy across the River, that the British forces were commanded by Col. Ennis [sic, Alexander Innis],

Daniel Chandler (S32175)
Regiment commanded by Colonel John Thomas, and of which Ben. Roebuck was lieutenant colonel or major. They were called South Carolina refugees and marched back through Charlotte in North Carolina to the Catawba and Broad Rivers in South Carolina, with a view to annoy the British and Tories, who then had possession of the whole state and this applicant remained in service, after thus again entering it, until this end of the war, for the first few months under the officers last above named, with whom he was in the battle with the British and Tories under Colonel Ferguson at the Cedar Springs, and also the battle near Musgrove's Mill on the Enoree River. Some little time after these engagements, they made their way down towards the lower end of the district of 96.

Mordecai Chandler (R1848)
I then fell in with Clarke and Shelby and was shortly afterwards at the battle at the Iron Works or Cedar Springs – and then at the battle of Musgrove's Mill– we then retreated to North Carolina.

Pharaoh Cobb (S1657)
We marched from the Watauga Settlements, and formed a junction with Col. McDowell near the Cherokee ford on Broad River. The men under Col. Shelby, Williams and Clark (sic, Clarke) were detached by Col. McDowell to act against a large body of Tories and British encamped at Musgrove's Mill on the south side of Enoree River. We

accordingly marched against them and had a battle with them on the 19th day of August 1780, which resulted in the defeat of the British and Tories, a number of them were killed and wounded, and a considerable number taken prisoners.

John Collins (S2848)
I then joined Col. Shelby and Col. Clark [sic, Elijah Clarke], and fought at the Battle of the Iron Works—and then took Thicketty Fort—I next fought at Musgroves Mill— and was ordered on to conduct the prisoners to North Carolina.

William Couch (R2361)
They remained there some time & returned to the upper Country & was at the battle of Blackstocks and also in a skirmish with the British at Musgrove's Mills.

Josiah Culbertson's Pension (S16354) does not mention Musgrove's Mill but he was evidently riding with Col. Shelby at that time.

Edward Doyle Pension Application (S32216)
..He joined a company on their march to Musgrove's Mill in ninety six District on the Enoree River and was at Said Mill engaged in a battle against the British and Tories—Col. Enis (sic, Innis) it was said Commanded the British Troops about one hundred and two hundred Tories—they were entirely Defeated. I saw fifty two dead bodies on the field of the Enemy—and among them was a British captain—it was said Col. Innis was wounded in the neck but made his escape. Our troops were commanded by Col. Williams, Col. Clark (sic, Elijah Clarke) and Col. Shelby in all about two hundred in this Battle. We had three men killed and but few wounded. This deponent was himself wounded slightly on the knuckle of the little finger of the left hand—we then took charge of the prisoners about twenty in number.

Potter Enloe (Inlow, Inloe) (W11912), applied by his widow.

Served until the close of the war and was in the battles of Musgrove's Mills, Blackstocks, Kings Mountain, Cowpens, Eutaw Springs and others not recollected and that his services were long and arduous and duly appreciated by the community.

Ebenezer Fain (R3421)

We then set out to meet the promised reinforcements from the British Army and met them at a place called Musgrove's Mill. Had an engagement with them and drove them back with considerable loss to them. They took shelter in the mill, barn and dwelling houses where we left them.

Lafford French (W7329)

..his next service was under Col. Thomas, a son of the first mentioned Colonel Thomas—we marched from King's Creek to York District South Carolina to Musgrove's Mills on Enoree and were joined on the way by Col. Clarke and he thinks Col. Shelby at the Mills we had a skirmish with a body of Tories whom we defeated killing a number and taking a number of prisoners how many he does not now recollect nor can he recollect the day or month but it was not long after his first service. He was not, he thinks, among whom I was one rendezvoused at Mountain Creek in Rutherford County waiting the return of Col. Clarke from Salisbury where he had gone with the prisoners taken at Musgroves Mills.

Robert Gilliam (Gillam, Gilam) (W8848) Application by his widow.

..he was also at the Battle of Musgrove's Mills and at the Battle of Blackstocks in South Carolina, and he was also at the Battle of the Cowpens in South Carolina, in these several Battles, her husband served as a private, but cannot state the names of the Captains, or Colonels, under whom he served in these several Battles.

David Golightly (S18888)
..was at the taking of Thicketty Fort; was at the battle of Musgrove's ford, and acted as a Lieutenant at the siege of Augusta.

William Goodlett (W8857)
That in the year 1780 he joined Capt. John Collins' Company, in the Regiment commanded by Col. John Thomas Junior and was in the Battle at Musgrove's Mills in August 1780:

McKeen Greene (W7561)
We joined Colonel Clark [sic, Elijah Clarke] and stayed there a month; and then marched to Sappril's [? Supprie's?] fort on Enoree River where we had a hot engagement with the British and Tories under Col. Innis where we killed him and defeated his forces, which consisted of 450 man. We then received an express that General Gates [Horatio Gates] was defeated at Camden and Colonel Sumter near Camden by Talton [sic, Banastre Tarleton] and that we must fly for our lives; we then fled to the upper part of North Carolina and joined Colonel McDole or Dowel [sic, Charles McDowell] near Broad River and stayed there five or six days.

Samuel Hammond (S21807)
In August 18 or 19 was with Col. Williams of Carolina, Clark of Georgia & Col. Shelby from over the mountains in the Battle of Musgrove's Mills on Enoree River 96 District. The Enemy were defeated, Col. Innis commanding officer of British wounded, Major Fraser 2nd in command killed, a number of prisoners taken who were committed to Applicant's Care & Safety. Conveyed to Hillsborough N.Carolina. While at that place received the appointment of Major with a Brevet.

Robert Henderson (S31738)

The next engagement took place between a party of our Regiment and the British and Tories at Musgrove's Mill on the Enoree River. I was not in this engagement being out with another party scouting in this engagement. We took about 30 prisoners. I was then sent as one of the guard to take the prisoners to Salisbury North Carolina. Colonel Williams of Laurens District South Carolina was the officer in charge of the prisoners.

Jacob Holman (R5265)

..Newberry district there remained six months keeping down the Tories; from thence to Musgrove's battle in Lawrence [sic, Laurens] district in the state aforesaid had an engagement with the British.

David Hughes (S2637)

That in the next year he was drafted for a three months tour to go South against the British under Captain Valentine Sevier, of Colonel Shelby's command, and rendezvoused in what is now Carter County, and marched across the Yellow mountains and entered the South and found other troops from the South under Cleveland, and had an engagement with the British at Eneree River, from which the troops were discharged by Colonel Shelby and returned home having fulfilled their term of service and discharge was verbal.

Joseph Hughes (S31764)

He was then soon after in the Battle at Musgrove's Mill & King's Mountain. Col. Clarke of Georgia commanded at Musgrove's & Capt. Shad Inman was killed. He received 7 shots from the Tories at King's Mountain. General Williams [James Williams] of S. Carolina was killed after the British raised the flag to surrender by a fire from some Tories.

William Kenedy (S2695)
....*he was at the Battle of Musgrove's Mills [sic, Musgrove Mill] under Capt. Joseph Hughes and Col. Brandon [Thomas Brandon];*

Isaac Lawrence (or Larence) (S32373)
In a short time after I volunteered I was in a two-days scrimmage or battle at Musgrove's Mill in South Carolina under Col. Williams....when I volunteered intending to go during the War, I was from [age] fourteen years Old in frequent scrimmages with the Tories.

Moses Lindsay (S4551)
We then went up to the ahead of Broad River and lay a short time. General Clarke then having the command of us in place of General Sumter who went to Salisbury for the purpose of healing his wounds and hearing [that a] considerable body of British and Tories had collected at Musgrove's Mill, marched us upon them and attacking them about the break of day we completely routed and defeated them. We then returned back to the edge of North Carolina to Gilbert Town where we lay until General Sumter having recovered of his wound resumed the command of us militia (which generally consisted of from three to 500 men) and General Clarke returned to Georgia.

Samuel Mayes (W2140)
He afterwards attached himself to the same Col. [to wit, Thomas Brandon], who had united his regiment with that of a Col. Williams of Ninety Six, South Carolina, while under their command he was in the battle at Musgrove's Mill, on Enoree River in the same District; the enemy being composed of British & Tories, commanded principally by one Col. Enos [sic, Innis], A British officer.

John Danal ...McDaniel (R6674)
Whilst here he was engaged in the Battle of Musgrove's Mill. The enemy (indecipherable word) on the attack, but were repulsed with considerable loss.

Joseph McJunkin (S18111)
We attacked & defeated after marching all night when we were about 540 Strong. I then fell under the Command of Col. Williams & hearing at Smith's ford that the British & Tories were encamped at Musgrove's Mill on Enoree River marched 40 miles that night & attacked the Tories as day broke and defeated them on 20th August 1780, and at the Close of this action we received Word that both Sumpter & Gates were defeated, which Caused us to abandon the Idea of Crossing the River to attack the British; having passed Ferguson's on our right we retreated towards the mountains.

William McKnight (S32407)
That he was engaged in the battles of Musgrove's Mill and King's Mountain with several other skirmishes of new note or importance. That he did not serve under Captain Parsons all the time, but occasionally under several other officers whose names he does not now recollect nor does he recollect who commanded at Musgrove's Mill. That at the battle of King's Mountain he was commanded by Colonel Williams who was wounded there and after died.

Michael Massengill (S1687)
In the month of July 1780, we marched under Captain Bean in the regiment commanded by Cols Clark [sic, Elijah Clarke], Shelby [Isaac Shelby] and Williams [James Williams] against a large party of Tories and British encamped at Musgrove Mills, on the south side of Enoree River, where we had a battle with them on 19th day of August 1780, which resulted in the defeat of the British and Tories, a number of them were killed and wounded and a considerable number were taken prisoners. This applicant

was in that battle and in that expedition he served about three months.

Notly Masters (W5365) Filed by his widow.
..was a private in the war of the Revolution and entered the service in South Carolina and was at the Battle at Musgrove's Mill, and she thinks he was under General Cazy (sic, Levi Casey?) and recollects to have heard her husband speak of being in several battles.

John Mills (S9024)
He recollects particularly being in an engagement at Musgroves Mills on the Enoree while serving under Captain Harris in which engagement he recollects a British soldier by the name of Mitchell was taken prisoner most of the enemy being Tories.

Hugh Moore (Moor) (W8473)
He then marched down on Enoree River and was engaged in the battle at Musgrove's Mill under the command of Clarke and Shelby [Isaac Shelby]. General McDowell having refused to cross the time (sic) of North, and march into South Carolina, remained in the first named state. When the battle of Musgrove's Mill was the fought, Col. Thomas was further down in South Carolina. Col Enis [sic, Alexander Innis] (or some such name) commanded the British at this engagement. They were defeated and lost about 200 men, killed and wounded, and about 90 prisoners. He marched and counter marched awhile in the States of North and South Carolina, being then under the command of Clarke (Shelby having remained in North Carolina).

Levi Mote (S7245)
...joined Col. Shelby and Col. Sevier and marched with them to Musgroves Mills and was in that Battle and at the expiration of three months was Discharged.

Matthew Nail (Neal) (S14004)

Affiant volunteered under Genl Clarke (Elijah Clarke) from Georgia who passed through our neighborhood with about two hundred men. When Genl Clarke left the neighborhood, he marched to the Enoree River in order to attack a band of British and Tories who were stationed there. We were interrupted before daylight by some of their spies. At daylight we charged on some of the spies and picket guard in which we were successful and took some prisoners. We kept the field and while we were remaining under arms we were attacked by some of the British and Tories from the station & fought with the fearful odds with about four to one against us but we were again successful & killed & took about a hundred of the British and Tories. After taking the prisoners to the barracks, being worn down & naked I got leave to visit my brother on the Nolichucky (river) over the mountains to get some clothes and to recruit myself.

Matthew Patton (S18153)

They were out until the first of May following. They were then ordered by Genl. Williamson to repair to their several regiments and in August 1780, he was at the Battle of Musgroves [sic, Musgrove's Mill].

Alexander Peden (S21417)

In North Carolina they met with Colonel McDowell's regiment but returned into South Carolina again and immediately afterwards was in the battle of "Musgrove's Mill." this tour & time of considerable importance are on Enoree River.

He resided in Spartanburg district South Carolina when he entered the service of his country. He volunteered in all five of the tours which he served. He was injured in the battles of Musgrove's Mill and two others with the Tories on Enoree River.

Samuel Peden (S30649)
May thereafter I was brevetted as a captain and served as such under the same command and was stationed near the Broad River, and marched to Musgrove's Mill and there had a Scrimmage with the British and Tories.

Henry Pettit (W5548)
We had many a chase after them. My next service was when Ferguson & Dunlap marched their Army through South Carolina into North Carolina. On their passage they was met by the Americans at Brown Old [?] fields. There were several killed. I was sent from that place with an express to Col. McDowell to Reinforce us. We pursued them after being reinforced to Musgrove's Mill on the Inoree [sic, Enoree] River where we overtook them and defeated them, In this service I was under Capt. James Smith, Col. John Thomas Commanded us.

William Prewett (R8460)
Sometime in the month of May a few days after the British took Charleston we left Ninety Six and marched to a place called Bunkers Hill and marched from there to the Musgrove Ford on the Enoree River and there had a scrimmage with the Tories and defeated them.

Samuel Quinton (S32461)
That the said Samuel Quinton, Senior, resided in what is now "Union District" South Carolina, at the time of the War of the Revolution, and entered the service of the United States as a private under the command of Captain John Mapp of Colonel Fair's Regiment of South Carolina Militia and served about eighteen months at the close of the war, and was at the battle on the Enoree, near Musgrove's Mills.

Samuel Ridgeway (S4119)
The Army then marched in pursuit of the Indians and Tories to Tugaloo on ?Savany? Savannah River then

returned to a place called Musgroves Mills on Enoree River in South Carolina,

Gilbert Shaw (W3876)
That he was afterwards called out in the year 1780, he thinks in the summer, and marched in the company of Captain Patton from Union District to Musgrove's Mill on the Enoree River, here under command of General Sumpter [sic, Thomas Sumter], the principal commander, they met and fought a part of the British forces. This action was fought very early in the morning about sunrise. At this place he was shot [illegible word?] the right thigh by a musket ball.

William Smith (W22272)
Shortly after which the Battle of Musgrove's [Musgrove Mill] was fought, in which I was engaged and after Gates' defeat and the defeat of Sumter, we again retreated to North Carolina.......he was also in the battle at Musgroves Mill on Enoree. Sumter was not there but Colonels Clark, Williams commanded.
(This pension application is 13 pages long and is an interesting document.)

Henry Story (S32537)
About the first of May 1780 he volunteered as a private soldier in Capt. Matthew Patton's company under the command of Col. Thomas Brandon & served from that time until the conclusion of the war as sergeant. He states that the battles or engagements of any consequence that he was in during the time of his service were the following: The Battle with the British & Tories at Musgrove's Mill in South Carolina on the River called Enoree (spelled Inoree) under Colonels Shelby and Clarke;

Lewis Taylor Pension (S1728)
I was in a battle fought at Musgrove's, Enoree [River] commanded by Colonel's Clarke [Elijah Clarke] and Shelby [Isaac Shelby]. This battle was the fought against the British and Tories.

Abraham Toney (R10642)
He was engaged in the battle at the Iron Works [probably Wofford's Iron Works], Musgroves [Musgrove's Mill].

Dennis Tramel (Trammel, Trammell) (R10672)
From there we marched down to Musgrove's Mill upon Enoree River under the command of Col. Isaac Shelby (since Governor of the State of Kentucky) and Col. Clarke from Georgia where we attacked the British and Tories that were stationed there under the command of Col. Ennis or Maj Ennis and completely defeated them—taking a number of prisoners—after sending the prisoners across the mountain for safe keeping, the place not now remembered—we marched from there to Black Stock's ford on the Tyger.

William Wilbanks (R11508) Filed by his widow.
He was at home some times, but not often, he served also under Captain William Young in Colonel Thomas Brandon's Regiment, that they then lived in Union District S. C. that he marched much through North and South Carolina was in Skirmishes at Musgrove's Ford on Enoree [River.]

Nathan Williford (S32066)
He was then in several scouting parties but no battles of importance until the battle at Musgrove's middle on the Enoree River under General Elijah Clarke.

William Young (W10008)
In the command of Col. Brandon with the rank of Lieutenant of horse and was soon after promoted to the rank of Captain of Cavalry in which capacity he served until the

close of the war under the command of Col. Brandon in South Carolina and under Col. or General Miller of the State of Georgia and was almost constantly in service from the fall of Charleston until the summer or fall of 1783 and was in the following battles viz.: Battle of Briar Creek, Stono, Siege of Augusta, King's Mountain, siege of Ninety Six, battle of Musgrove's mill, battle of the Cowpens and many other skirmishes.

Additions to the pension site continue. Check

revwarapps.com

for updates.

CHAPTER ELEVEN

Musgrove's Mill in Print

Early historians focused their attention on major battles in the south and there was little attention paid to the militia engagements. It is fair to say that most of the country had no idea of the role the militia had played in thwarting Lord Cornwallis's ambitious campaign to take the South. It would be fiction writers who would first bring this theatre of the war to the attention of the reading public across the nation.

William Pendleton Kennedy published **Horse-Shoe Robinson: A Tale of Tory Ascendency** in 1835. Others were writing novels based on the Revolutionary War such as William Gilmer Simms who wrote on the events in the Low Country and focused on Francis Marion's command. Kennedy's work is included here because his novel addresses the conflict in the back country of South Carolina in general and the events in the area of the Enoree River in particular.

In 1816 Kennedy sat down with a veteran of the Revolutionary War who was noted among his neighbors as a great story-teller. Kennedy recorded the conversations and later wrote a novel depicting this American as a hero. The book was called **Horse-Shoe Robinson**. The book was reprinted several times and was widely read, the most popular Southern novel of the time. It was praised by such well-known authors as Edgar Allen Poe, who referred to it as "A book of no ordinary character" (Kennedy, 1735:xxvi).

The hero of the novel is Sergeant Galbraith Robinson who, as Kennedy explains, was a blacksmith before the war and is called Horse-Shoe. He is described as a very tall, rough, strong man able to withstand the rugged life of the times. He and a companion, Continental Army Captain Arthur Butler, move from Charleston across South Carolina attempting to reach Georgia and Colonel Elijah Clarke who was the commander of the Wilkes County Militia. Robinson and Butler become involved in the militia engagements in the back country.

It is difficult to determine in historic fiction what is history and what is fiction. Do the stories told to Kennedy contain important information about the war or are they merely a vehicle for a romantic novel of the period?

Although one can never be sure, it is important to look at the credentials of the source, the man Kennedy calls Horse-Shoe Robinson. He was, in fact, a veteran of the American Revolution whose name was James Robertson. His pension application is available (See: James Robertson, S14341). He enlisted from Union County into the 6th Regiment of South Carolina Provincials and later enlisted in the Continental Army for three years. He eventually was in the 1st Regiment of South Carolina.

According to his pension application, Robertson was at the Battle of Stono and at the attempt of the Americans and French to retake Savannah. When Charleston fell, Private James Robertson was taken prisoner and interned at Fort Moultrie, Sullivan's Island. After a month he was able to escape and evidently made his way back to Union County where he enlisted in Thomas Brandon's militia. It appears he spent the remainder of the war as militia in the Backcountry. Since Brandon fought at Musgrove's Mill, King's Mountain, Blackstock's and Cowpens, it is possible that Robertson was engaged in at least some of that action if not all of it. He only mentions Cowpens in his pension application.

Although Kennedy refers to Horse-Shoe as a sergeant, there is no evidence that he ever advanced beyond the rank of private. Also, it is improbable that he was a blacksmith. After the war he settled on the horse-shoe bend of the Chauga River and, by the time Kennedy had encountered him, he was known as "Horse-Shoe" to distinguish him among other Robertson settlers in the area. (Information supplied by John Robertson, a descendent of James Robertson).

The story begins with the narration of how Horse-Shoe escaped from Charleston, and then his travels with Butler through the back country. Are all the incidents accurate? Probably not. It is likely that James Robertson embellished his service as he related it to Kennedy. Perhaps Kennedy embellished the information he was given in order to write the novel. What is remarkable about the story is that it was written at all. It was a daring move on Kennedy's part to write of the treachery and brutality of a fratricidal war.

When the book was published in 1838, James Robertson was an old man, living in Tuskaloosa, Alabama. Kennedy arranged to have the book read to Robertson who was illiterate. After the reading Robertson is reported to have remarked: *"It is all true and right-in its right place—excepting about them women, which I disremember. That mought be true too: but my memory is treacherous-I disremember"* (Kennedy, 1838:10).

There are two women in this romantic story which portrays two couples in love. One couple will survive and live happily ever after. The other couple will be separated by death. The latter is the story of a miller's daughter, Mary Musgrove, who lives with her family on the Enoree River. Her father is described as a pious older man who laments the fact that the British force him to grind their wheat without pay and billet their officers in his house without invitation. Mary is an avowed Patriot and is involved in the intrigue which was typical of life in the area.

The Musgrove Mill site figures prominently in the story and the battle fought there is only one of the many events included in the novel. Many of the details Kennedy includes are accurate but some are in error. He identifies Shelby, Williams and Clarke as protagonists, and Colonel Innes as the British commander. However, the battle in the novel is fought by mounted militia. Whether that is the way Robertson reported it or Kennedy interpreted it is a matter of conjecture. In the novel Williams and Clarke collect the prisoners and move north with them before separating, and that is accurate.

Mary smuggles messages to the Continental officer, Captain Butler, who is imprisoned in her house. She arranges for the escape of the prisoner and in this incident, Mary's lover, a local militia man, is killed by the Tories.

Although the author then moves the action to the other heroine who is accompanied south from Virginia by Horse-Shoe, he takes considerable literary license with the facts. It is highly unlikely that James Robertson ever had a face-to-face conversation with Lt. Col. Banastre Tarleton.

Returning to the conflict in the back country of South Carolina, the author accurately relates Clarke's attack on Augusta and his exodus from there with his civilians. The attempt of Ferguson to intercept Clarke is also a correct interpretation of the events.

When Horse-Shoe is reunited with Mary Musgrove and her father, he finds that they have been forced from their home which had been burned by Tories in retaliation for their Patriot activities. Mr. Musgrove had sent his wife and younger children ahead to relatives in Virginia, and he and Mary are traveling north to join them. This story of the burned house has been passed down in the Musgrove's family but it is uncertain whether Kennedy had this information from a reliable source, or whether it is part of the fiction which the family assumed was accurate.

The two heroines of the story, Mary Musgrove and Mildred Lindsey, meet and from this point to the end of the novel, they will remain together and become fast friends. Accompanied by Horse-Shoe, they will pursue Ferguson who now has Mildred's love, Capt. Butler, as prisoner. The unfortunate Butler had been recaptured after his escape from the Musgrove home. This rather contrived arrangement allows the three to follow Ferguson to King's Mountain and the conclusion of the story.

Kennedy mentioned no other source than Robinson. However, his descriptions of the events leading up to the battle at King's Mountain contain considerable information which is absolutely accurate. He mentioned the two commanders of the thirty Georgians that Clarke sends to accompany the militia: Major Chandler (actually, Candler) and Captain Johnson. In addition he included several militia leaders who had assembled, and the chase to King's Mountain. He correctly described Col. Williams's death at the end of the battle.

The value of the book is that readers across the country became acquainted with what had happened in the backcountry of South Carolina. It includes the militia engagements which led up to the battle at King's Mountain, including the battle at Musgrove's Mill.

There were local scholars who were working to gather information on the war in the back country of South Carolina. John M. Logan, A.M., published his first volume of **A History of the Upper Country of South Carolina from the Earliest Periods to the Close of the War of Independence** in 1859. His intention was to provide a text of the history of South Carolina for high school students. The first volume is a treasure for those seeking information about the early Indian culture. There are extensive descriptions of hunting techniques, preserving game, smelting metals, and a wealth of information on Indian slavery. The book is rich in the activities of the early settlers, and includes much interesting information about those families.

One intriguing section addresses the possible locations of the lost mines which, according to the legends, were known to the Indians and hidden from the white settlers and lost forever.

The volume covers a series of incidents involving traders and Indians and the abuses in that trade which led to conflicts in the back country. Also, he covers the extensive negotiating between Gov. Glen and the Indian chiefs in an attempt to maintain peace in the face of deteriorating relations between the disaffected Indians and the settlers. The volume ends with the following:

"And now the trail of events begins rapidly to transpire, which were to prove the proximate cause of inflicting upon Upper Carolina the horrors of another Indian war. This war was the Cherokee war of 1760; but its story of carnage, and thrilling scenes of savage vengeance on the border, must be reserved for another volume" (Logan, 1859:355).

Logan had planned a second volume which was to have covered the Revolutionary War. To this purpose, he had been gathering information for over twenty years before the publication of the first volume. He had interviewed veterans of the Revolutionary War and recorded their conversations. However, the War Between the States interrupted his writing and he served as a Surgeon in the Confederate Army. Following the war he resumed his medical career on the faculty of Atlanta Medical College. He died on March 29, 1885, without ever writing the second volume. Dr. Logan is buried in Greenwood, South Carolina.

When Dr. Logan moved from South Carolina he left his notes with his father-in-law, Dr. E. R. Calhoun. When Lyman Draper was researching for his work on King's Mountain, he copied Dr. Logan's notes and much of that information is in the Draper book. The original notes have been lost, but in 2009, Pelham Lyle and Val Greene of Fairfield County Museum, published one volume containing a reprint of Logan's first volume, and the reconstructed notes taken by Draper and others.

Although Logan's excellent work has been used to good effect by others, it is a great loss that he did not write the volume as he intended. When Logan interviewed the Revolutionary War veterans, he knew many of them and often included notes on their families, their in-laws and their neighbors.

Historian Dr. Bobbie Gilmer Moss and cartography John Robertson often expound on the fact that terrain determined where and how battles were fought in the backcountry. Dr. Logan knew the terrain. He knew the roads the militia had taken, the fords they had crossed, the fields in which they had camped and the sites on which they had fought. He had walked that territory and had examined King's Mountain in the company of his grandfather who had fought there.

One has only to read Volume One with its wealth of information and detail to imagine what Logan could have written and lament the fact that we have missed a great work.

The War Between the States not only interrupted Dr. Logan's writing, but turned the nation's attention to a new conflict. At the conclusion of that war, people had a far different response to it than they had to the Revolution. These battles were not forgotten. Monuments were built on battlefields, veterans were honored in parades and historians hastened to document the battles and record every aspect of the war. However, there were those who had not forgotten the debt owed to the men who had fought for independence.

In 1881, Dr. Lyman C. Draper published **Kings Mountain and Its Heroes**, based on correspondence with families of participants, families who lived in the area of the battles, pension records and written accounts. Although published one hundred and one years after the battle, he had started his research in 1839 and had interviewed three veterans of the battle. As mentioned previously, he had copied the research of Dr. Logan of South Carolina and included much of that work, especially in the chapter of the battle at Musgrove's Mill.

Draper's work had a wide circulation and served to direct attention again to the events of the Revolutionary War. The more recent War Between the States had focused the attention of the nation on that war. Now Draper's work again reminded readers of the debt owed those who had fought for independence.

In 1897, Dr. J. B. O. Landrum published **Colonial and Revolutionary History of Upper South Carolina: Embracing for the most part the primitive and colonial history of the territory comprising the original county of Spartanburg with a general review of the entire military operations in the upper portion of South Carolina and portions of North Carolina.**

Landrum's intentions are clearly expressed in the Preface:

"Most of our most interesting past being now scattered in books long since gone out of publication, the author feels the force of suggestions made to him, that the time has come when that part deserving preservation should be made of convenient and lasting record. In no one work examined has he found a complete list of battles and skirmishes occurring in our immediate vicinity during the Revolutionary war. No record of this period tells of both the battles of Blackstock's and Musgroves, and yet they were fought within nine months of the same date, as well as within ten or twelve miles of the same point" (Landrum, 1897: i-ii).

Landrum addresses the period of Indian settlement briefly, referring the reader to Logan's more lengthy work. The colonial period includes an alphabetical listing of the families in the area as of 1785. This material is of considerable interest to families who trace their roots to the early settlers. Old forts and stockades are located with considerable accuracy in terms of the surrounding landmarks available in this period. Landrum grew up in the area and knew the roads and the terrain, as well as the families on whose property those sites were located. He includes notes and correspondence concerning sites of events and graves.

Landrum achieved what he was determined to accomplish. He relates the events in chronological order and in great detail. His treatment of Musgrove's Mill includes material from both Draper and Schenck, but his account of the battle itself is based on Hammond's report, not Shelby's as Draper had. He locates the graves of the casualties by property owners and church locations, a valuable resource for readers at that time.

The title, however, is misleading, as the work encompasses far more than a mere recitation of the back country militia events. Although focusing on the local history, Landrum puts the events in proper perspective in terms of the entire British campaign in the South.

Although Landrum's work was valuable for readers beyond Upper South Carolina, it evidently did not have a national appeal. Published in Greenville, South Carolina, it was possibly considered just a history of regional interest. It was soon out of print, and not reprinted until 1977.

It would appear that there was little understanding of the role played by the militia in the backcountry of the South during the Revolutionary War. In fact, there seem to be little interest in the Southern Campaign during the most of the twentieth century.

That would change with the seminal work of Dr. Henry Lumpkin, **From Savannah to Yorktown: The American Revolution in the South**, published in 1981. Dr. Lumpkin, on the faculty of The University of South Carolina, was an internationally known and respected military historian. He had hosted a public television program, *And Then There Were Thirteen*, which had been critically acclaimed and had aroused considerable enthusiasm not only among historians but also the general public. This new treatment of the Revolutionary War in the South was published in large format and in color, and included maps, illustrations, weapons, and uniforms. The same year it was printed in paperback and in black and white.

The Appendix in Lumpkin's book contains an annotated Chronology of the Revolution from 1775-1783, and an overview of the major battles fought in the south including units involved, commanders and casualties. As would be expected of a military historian, a chapter covers uniforms and weapons in great detail.

However, the strength of the book is the narrative of the British attempt to take the South. Addressing the Revolutionary War, Lumpkin begins with an account of the early years, noting:

"During the first two years of the Revolutionary War, Virginia, the Carolinas, and Georgia were torn by bitter fratricidal civil war between pro-British Loyalists and Americans supporting the cause of independence. Skirmishes, raids, and counterraids occurred, including a brutally successful frontier campaign against the Cherokee Indians and their royalist agents" (Lumpkin, 1981:10).

"Fighting between Patriot and Loyalist continued throughout the South. It was to be waged with increasing hatred and intensity – an unceasing, merciless internecine conflict the civilized British found difficult to comprehend and impossible to counter" (Lumpkin, 1981:6).

The British had been successful at Charleston and Camden and had established posts across the state from which British troops could operate. These posts also served as mustering points for Loyalist or Tory militia. However, the British did not control the vast, unsettled backcountry of the south. It was in this area that Patriot militia operated.

Who were these Patriots and why did they resist British occupation? Lumpkin explains:

"In a few short months the British had thoroughly antagonized and in many cases forced into open rebellion men who would have been quite content to remain at home as paroled prisoners of war. In the same period the British manage to shock, anger, and estrange large elements of the Scots-Irish Presbyterians and Welsh Baptists by attacking their churches, the very center of settlement life. The ruthless brutality of Tarleton undoubtedly created a sense of fear, although most South Carolinians and Georgians simply became angry and vengeful.

"The hard, dour, Scot-Irish Calvinists, the Welsh Baptists, the Huguenot and English planters now took the field with Francis Marion, Thomas Sumter, Elijah Clarke, and William Davies. It was impossible to intimidate by fiat or force men schooled in the ultimate harshness of Indian warfare and frontier life" (Lumpkin, 1981:250).

In the months following the fall of Charleston, Patriot militia engaged in a series of attacks and skirmishes. For every one Patriot casualty, they had inflicted three casualties on British Regulars and Provincials and their Loyalist supporters. In these encounters Lord Cornwallis lost 500 of the 4000 troops he commanded in South Carolina, and the Patriot victories also intimidated many of the British supporters in the area.

Along with details of the campaigns of Francis Marion and Thomas Sumter, Lumpkin covers additional engagements in **The Fighting Partisans of the Backcountry.** The action began on July 12 with Patriot militia killing Captain Huck and soldiers of the British Legion at Williamson's Plantation in the York district, and Colonel John Thomas turning back a Loyalist attack at Cedar

Springs near Spartanburg. Attacks continued at Gowen's Old Fort, Earle's Ford and Fort Prince.

"These were not big engagements, but they began to hurt. The British and Loyalists had lost more than 100 men in five days, while the American partisan casualties were less than half that number" (Lumpkin, 1981: 83).

The fighting continued through July and into August. Among the engagements covered is the Battle of Musgrove's Mill.

"A savage and hot little action fought at Musgrove's Mill, South Carolina, on 17 August (sic) was a clear American victory but could not mitigate the double disasters of Camden and Fishing Creek. Learning that a strong body of Loyalists were posted at Musgrove's Mill on the south side of the Enoree River, Colonel Elijah Clarke with his Georgians, Colonel James Williams leading South Carolinians, and Colonel Isaac Shelby, who had joined Clarke with a contingent of wild frontier riflemen from the Watauga settlements in what is now Tennessee, determined to attack Musgrove's Mill. In the early morning of 18 August, 200 well-armed and well-mounted American partisans arrived about a mile of Musgrove's Mill" (Lumpkin, 1981:87).

The narrative continues with a description of the battle, and of the events following Musgrove's Mill, leading up to the American victory at King's Mountain,

"the first major step in the two-year campaign that led to Cornwallis's surrender at Yorktown and the final expulsion of the British from Georgia and the Carolinas" (Lumpkin, 1981:104).

There is one weakness in the publication. Although there is a bibliography which is divided among categories addressed, there are no citations in the body of the work. In spite of this, it is fair to say that Dr. Lumpkin legitimized the role of the Patriot militia and afforded them considerable credit in thwarting the British advance in the South.

Since the publication of Lumpkin's work, other scholars have addressed the British campaign in the South with varying degrees of credit for the militia. However, for our purposes, the most detailed accounts of the militia engagements in the Backcountry are found in **The Road to Guilford Courthouse** by John Buchanan, published in 1997. An accomplished writer and meticulous researcher, Buchanan covers only the events till March of 1781 in a volume of 450 pages. The narrative reads like a novel with background information, biographical information on the participants and vivid descriptions of the events of the period. However, research on which the work is based is cited throughout, with an additional annotated bibliography.

For our purposes, most important are the chapters *"More Trouble in the Back Country,"* which covers the events prior to the Battle of Camden, and *"The Partisans Fight On,"* which covers the battles following Camden and leading to King's Mountain. Of the Battle of Musgrove's Mill Buchanan writes:

"The British defeat was complete, and this did not bode well for the Tory cause. In the middle of strong Tory country a small band of daring Rebel guerillas had badly hurt and sent flying in disarray regulars and militia more than double their number. The British loss was sixty-three killed, ninety wounded, seventy taken prisoner, a total out of 223 out of Innes's combined force of 500. The Rebels lost four killed and seven wounded. They were elated" (Buchanan, 1997:179).

However, when news of Gates's defeat at Camden arrived, the commanders, Shelby, Clarke and Williams, were forced to retreat, abandoning a raid on the British post at Ninety-Six.

"Isaac Shelby proposed that all concerned consider raising an army from the Over Mountain men and the Back Country militia to deal with Ferguson....

"Gates may have lost most of his army but they (the militia) had won their fight, and they were not prepared to surrender the Back Country to the King's Inspector of Militia, Major Patrick Ferguson" (Buchanan, 1997: 179-180).

And they didn't. They settled their score with Ferguson at King's Mountain.

With a new interest in Revolutionary War sites, South Carolina endeavored to search out and erect historical markers. However, when the **South Carolina Highway Historical Marker Guide** was published in 1998, there was no historical marker to designate the site of the Battle of Musgrove's Mill.

How could it have been overlooked? Would Musgrove's Mill forever be forgotten?

CHAPTER TWELVE

History Reclaimed

Early land records indicate that Edward Musgrove owned 250 acres on the south side of the Enoree River. He had been a surveyor and had drawn up the plat for Samuel Chew's plat across the Enoree, and was familiar with the area (Hiatt, 2000).

A wagon road crossed the Enoree at a ford east of Cedar Shoals Creek. For a settler with plans to build a mill, the site was ideal. The ford, as well as the mill, would become known as Musgrove's.

The Musgrove family had survived the war, and by the time of Edward's death in 1790, he had apparently built a prosperous business. In his will he referred to his property as a plantation (Hiatt, 2000). In addition to his mill, he owned five slaves and other household property.

Family records indicate that the two oldest daughters, Mary and Susan remained unmarried and died of consumption (tuberculosis). There is a suggestion in the genealogical record that they died shortly after the war. They evidently predeceased their father as there is no mention of them in the will. Edward Musgrove left money to his oldest son, Edwards Beaks Musgrove, and to two married daughters, Rebecca Cameron and Mary (Merry, Marrey) Berry. The mill property and adjoining land was left to his son, William, with the provision that Edward's widow, Ann (Nancy Ann) would retain ownership and profits during her

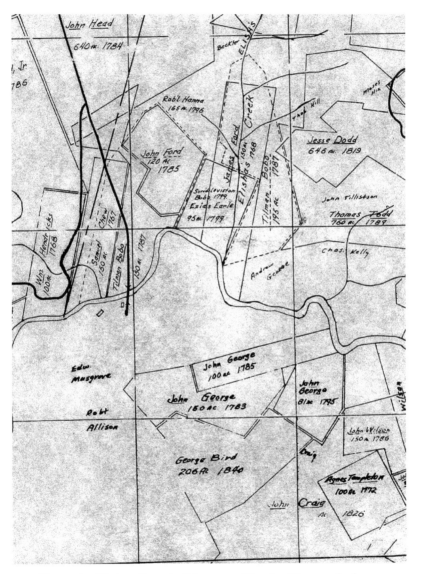

From the Union County Museum. Used with permission.

life (Hiatt, 2000). According to the plat she bought a section of property in her own right in 1791.

Edward Musgrove left a profitable estate.

"At the time of his death, Musgrove owned 8 head of cattle, 29hogs, and 16 geese. He also owned 3 horses....Other implements and goods enumerated in the inventory indicate that Musgrove devoted a majority of his tilled land to the cultivation of corn, but he also raised significant quantities of flax (for making linen) and cotton, and even kept beehives, presumably for the production of honey and wax. ...The presence of the mill, however, suggests that its proprietor grew corn, and possibly even wheat, on a commercial basis. Musgrove doubtlessly earned additional money by grinding the grains of other local planters at his gristmill" (Hiatt, 2000).

In spite of the estate Edward Musgrove had left, the family did not continue to prosper. Ann Musgrove remarried a David Smith who became indebted to a neighbor, George Gordon. When Ann's property was not sufficient to pay the debt, the mill property was confiscated by Gordon in 1796. The mill became known as Gordon's Mill as is indicated in early maps of the region, but the ford continued to be known as Musgrove's.

In 1840, after Gordon's death, William Musgrove purchased back the property which his father had intended him to have. By then the tract was 318 acres (Hiatt, 2000). During this period a toll bridge spanned the Enoree River, at the site of the ford on William Musgrove's property.

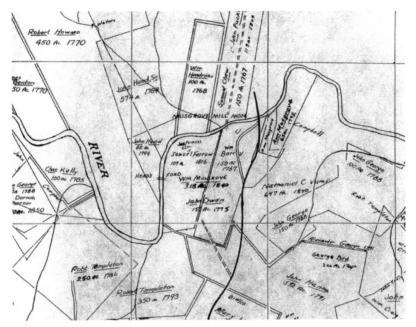

From the Union County Museum. Used with permission.

The above plat shows William Musgrove's property. It is of a later period and has been notated over the years. However, it does indicate that William owned the original mill property.

One interesting addition to the plat is the notation "MUSGROVE MILL MON." on the north side of the Enoree. The date it was added is unknown but, at some period, there must have been some recognition of the battle.

When William died in 1848 the property included a sawmill, and a forge. His inventory included 18 slaves, 30 head of cattle, 38 swine, 6 goats and 4 mules. Produce listed as 3,000 pounds of pork, 700 bushels of corn 200 bushels of wheat and picked cotton as well as crops of potatoes, turnips and cabbage unharvested (Hiatt, 2000).

The property passed to his nephew, Edward Bobo who made significant improvements. However, after four years a flood washed away the mills.

In 1859 the property was purchased by Lewis Yarborough and was held by him until his death in 1897 when R. C. Burnett acquired the property.

In the early 1900's Burnett sold the property to the Thornwell Orphanage and the house, known as the Musgrove House, was used for the family of the manager of the farm.

In July of 1911, a group of ladies from the Musgrove Mill Chapter of the Daughters of the American Revolution visited the property accompanied by Mrs. L. D. Childs, a descendent of Edward Musgrove. This gives another intriguing twist to the Musgrove story. Mrs. Childs, also a member of the DAR, traces her ancestry to Edward Musgrove through a daughter, Ann, born of "third wife Adair," and born in 1773 while he was married to Nancy Ann Musgrove. There is speculation that this "third wife, Anne Adair" is really Nancy Ann Musgrove and the birth record was in error. Nancy Ann may have been connected to the Adairs, or previously married to an Adair, a common name in the area. An interesting aside is that in Kennedy's Horseshoe Robinson, Mary is first introduced at the home of her uncle, Nat Adair, who we will come to learn is a traitor. Did Kennedy's informant know of a connection between the Musgrove family and Adair or is it just a coincident? In any case, daughter Anne married Absolam Bobo, and Mrs. Childs was Bessie Springs Bobo before her marriage.

On that July day the ladies were searching for the grave of Mary Musgrove of Horseshoe Robinson fame. The grave was reported to be about 100 yards from the house and the ladies located the site to their satisfaction and a stone marker has been erected at that site.

Marker for Mary Musgrove

Mrs. Childs wrote of the house:

"The house has an ideal situation on a prominence overlooking the Enoree river at a point once known as the Horse Shoe Bend, where a long bridge connects with the opposite shore, rising in mountainous peaks. From whence we stood we could command a view of three counties, Spartanburg, Union and Laurens, and see the smoke of factory chimneys in four distant towns. Down almost beneath us nestled the mill, so well known in history, its wheel turned now by the same power which turned it during the Revolutionary war, in which it figured. A grove of cedar trees formed a beautiful setting for the houses and there old-fashioned flowers, which must have been planted

generations ago, are still struggling for existence" (Childs, 1911).

Unfortunately the house was abandoned about 1960 and burned in 1971 (Hiatt, 2000).

As the bicentennial of American Independence approached, there was a renewed interest in the Revolutionary War battles across the country. In South Carolina, an American Revolution Bicentennial Commission was established with Samuel P. Manning as Vice-chair. He was a long-time history enthusiast and an ardent preservationist, and represented Spartanburg County in the South Carolina House of Representatives from 1967 to 1982.

The commission started its work in the late 1960's and Manning was determined to ensure that not only South Carolina but the nation would gain new understanding of South Carolina's role in the founding of the nation.

"There were 130 major battles fought in South Carolina during the Revolution, and most of those sites are either undeveloped or worse, unmarked" (Manning, in *The Columbia Record*, 23 Dec. 1969).

He worked tirelessly to commemorate the events at Cowpens and Eutaw Springs. Although the Cowpens battle site was recognized as a National Battlefield, Eutaw Springs remained neglected until well after Manning's death. However, his dedication to preserving South Carolina's history was productive. In 1975 the South Carolina Department of Parks, Recreation and Tourism bought the 330.39 acres of the Musgrove Mill tract from the Thornwell Orphanage (Hiatt, 2000).

Manning's address on the occasion of the purchase of the property was inspirational. He not only reiterated the details of the battle but commented on the lives of many of the participants and their contributions to building the nation after the war. Since that material is not available to the reader in one place, the address in its entirety in included in Appendix II.

Manning believed, as did others, that the purchase included property on both sides of the Enoree River. It did not. The property was all on the south side of the Enoree where the Musgroves had their home and where the British had encamped. However, those 330+ acres were protected but, due to lack of funding, were not developed as an historic site as Manning had hoped. Historians and locals hiked the property and hoped for an eventual permanent site.

One of the frequent visitors to the area was Dr. George Fields, a local historian and a long-time champion of the Musgrove Mill battle site. In 1997 he realized that the property on the north side of the Enoree was not state-owned and was being sectioned for sale for housing. He revealed that his thought was how can we lose a rural site between the Enoree River and Cross Anchor?

A frequent hiker in the area, he had observed that the iron marker designating the battlefield had disappeared in recent years, and the stone marker for Shadrick Inman's grave had been moved. Was there a way to protect and preserve this important site?

The first approach was to Ken Driggers of the Palmetto Conservation Foundation, an organization in which Dr. Fields was active. Although interested in preserving this site, that organization was totally committed financially to another project. However, there were locals who felt strongly that the property should be saved. Early supporters of the efforts were Donny Wilder, South Carolina Representative from Clinton, and historian Colonel William Jackson "Jack" Whitener of Union, guaranteeing the support of Laurens and Union Counties. To raise money to purchase the property targeted for development, the Spartanburg County Foundation was formed. The membership of the committee to move the project forward is listed in Appendix III. Funds were raised and the property was purchased and ceded to

South Carolina Department of Parks, Recreation and Tourism (SCPRT). Musgrove Mill would be a South Carolina State Historic Site with Frank Stovall as park manager. The members of SCPRT who contributed to this effort are listed in Appendix III.

Laurens County built a road into the site, and volunteers built the split-rail fence along the entrance road. Boys Scouts built a roadside kiosk by the Highway 56 bridge. The site received public, private and corporation support and the project moved along. Development continued with a visitors' center, housing for the manager, trails, as well as the infrastructure. This was accomplished by SCPRT Central Maintenance and Construction Team whose names are listed in Appendix III.

The week-end before the public dedication, re-enactors mustered at the site. Backcountry militia of the South Carolina Rangers mingled with uniformed British soldiers, examining weapons and talking midst the music of drummers and fifers. Period costumed women and children worked at their spinning wheels, or cooked over the open fires. A dream had been realized. The site of the Battle of Musgrove's Mill had been reclaimed and was now open for all to appreciate.

The first week-end of May 2003, dignitaries assembled to celebrate this new tribute to history: Musgrove Mill State Historic Site. The speakers' stand was on the porch at the front of the Visitor Center, facing the site of the original Musgrove house. In a moving ceremony, beneath a Carolina blue sky, Van Stickles, Director of Parks for South Carolina Parks, Recreation and Tourism, presented Representative Donny Wilder with a framed Resolution of Appreciation for his work in preserving the site. A portrait of Representative Wilder hangs in the Visitor Center.

Visitor Center with the Musgrove house site in the foreground.

Now, over 220 years after the battle had been fought on the banks of the Enoree River, its place in South Carolina's Revolutionary War history had been established.

CHAPTER THIRTEEN

The Present

Today the visitors at Musgrove Mill State Historic Site enjoy what Samuel Manning described as *"an area of picturesque beauty with rolling hills, thick woods, clean cool streams and river shoals"* (Manning, Appendix II).

The park encompasses two areas: the main property contains the Visitors Center close to the site of the Musgrove House which burned in 1970. Inside are displays to illustrate life in the backcountry as well as tributes to Mary Musgrove and Horseshoe Robinson.

The monument to Shadrick Inman, the hero of the battle, which once stood to mark his grave, is on view. Revolutionary War weapons line the walls. A light show will show the visitor how the battle was fought and won.

From the verandah surrounding the building, one can sit in a rocking chair and survey the landscape. One view overlooks the cleared land down to the Enoree River where British troops encamped, and where they marched off to battle, only to return in a rout with the Patriots shooting them down as they ran. Another view overlooks the area where the house once stood, and is now used as a mustering place for South Carolina Rangers who regularly gather to display frontier life and Revolutionary War tactics. Other events are planned by The Friends of Musgrove Mill, a group of supporters of the site.

View of slope from the Visitor Center down to the Enoree
River, where British troops were encamped.

Visitors can picnic, fish in the two-acre pond, or walk the
trails. Take time to visit the marker for Mary Musgrove's
grave which was erected by the Daughters of the American
Revolution.

From the banks of the Enoree River one can see the stone
footings of the old bridge which crossed the river from the
Musgrove property before the road (Highway 56) was
rerouted to the east of the property.

Also, from the banks of the Enoree, one can see the stone
foundations of the old mill which was destroyed when the
Enoree flooded.

The property on the north side of the Enoree River must
be approached by crossing the river on Highway 56. The site
includes a boat launch area for kayaks and small boats as
well as a picnic site.

The visitor may walk along Cedar Shoals Creek beside Horseshoe Falls where, Kennedy wrote, that Horseshoe Robinson hid from his British pursuers.

Horseshoe Falls

Today the sediment at the bottom of the falls makes that seem impossible. However, Dr. Fields, who has hiked the property frequently over the years, reports that he observed an interesting event.

Once, after torrential rains in the upstate flooded the rivers, he saw that the water rushing over the falls had flushed out the sediment at the foot of the falls clear to the rocky bed of the creek. He observed that, under those circumstances, there was sufficient room under the falls to have hidden a man. Could there have been such a cavern over two hundred years ago? Certainly the terrain changes over time with erosion from wind and water. Agriculture allowed more sediment to run off into the rivers. It does cause one to speculate.

Does all this mean that the report of Horseshoe Robinson hiding under the falls is true? Or could the falls have been used as a hiding place for other Revolutionary soldiers? Certainly not, but it does give the visitor another idea to ponder about the rich tradition of the place.

Today Musgrove Mill State Historic Site stands as a reminder of the early settlers who braved the frontier to establish homes in this wilderness. It also tells the story of militia from three states who moved against the British encampment and, although facing terrible odds, routed their enemy and gave heart to a struggling people. It also is a tribute to the endeavors of historians, politicians and local residents who were determined that the stories should not die and the battleground should be saved. Now, over 230 years after the battle, visitors can walk the historic ground and learn about South Carolina's rich Revolutionary War history.

APPENDIX I

Col. Daniel Clary's Dutch Fork Regiment drew British pounds for the period of 14 June to 13 December 1780. Those listed as receiving pay includes the following, most of whom may have been at Musgrove's Mill on August 19.

Captain Vachel Clary's Company

Lt. Joseph King
Quarter Master John Abbott
Ensign James Fay
Ensign Daniel Moffet

Privates:

Thomas Black	George King	David Flemming
William Golden	William Hubbs	James Knight
John Connell	Jesse Few	Curtis Hill
James Penney	Joseph Connell	Daniel Horsey
Nathaniel Keaton	William Moffitt	Benjamin Conwell
Alexander Stewart	George Clark	William McQueen
Daniel Regan	Jesse Davis	Reuben Morgan
Thomas Brown	John Griffin, Jr.	William Howell
William McConnel	John Elmore	Horatio Griffin
William Wyatt	William Connell	Jacob Odam
John Lester	Jones Wells	Jonathan White
John Davis	Thomas Gibson	Samuel Dunkin
John Pearson	George McKinney	James Lester
Lowdon Hensen	Benjamin James	William Elmore
David McNive	John Turner	Moses Smith
Phillip Hopkins	Enoch Smith	James McClain
Robert Gillam	James Summers	Archibald Slone
John McLeland	William McLeland	

Captain Humphrey Williamson's Company

Captain Humphrey Williamson
Lt. James Wilkerson
Captain William Ballentine (66 days pay)

Appendix I

Lt. Thomas Bee (66 days pay)
Ensign George Lightsee (66 days pay)

Privates:

Samuel Gregory	Jeremiah Gregory	Hendrey Snelgrove
Adam Priester	John Miller	Aaron Mills
Thomas Parkins	John Beeman	Thomas Smith
George McCullough	William Moore	Peter Leites

Joseph Arems (66 days pay)   Benjamin Gregory (66 days pay)
Jacob Oxner (66 days pay)

Captain George Stroup's Company

Captain George Stroup

Privates:
Ballentine Glassman, witness   Robert Blair
George Severly   John Stroup

Captain James Wright's Company

Captain James Wright

Privates;
John Herrin   Lawrence Richardson   Samuel Lanford

Captain John Cunningham's Company

Privates:

Thomas Brown (103 days pay)		William Cornwall
David Fleming, unpaid as of 14 March		Thomas Gibson
Robert Gilliam	Williams Hubbs	Nathaniel Heaton
Benjamin James	Reuben Morgan	David McNaver
James Penny	Daniel Ragan	Moses Smith
Enoch Smith	Archibald Stone	John Turner

Widow of Captain David Reece received pay for deceased husband.

Appendix I

Captain William Ballentine's Company

Captain William Ballentine
Lt. Thomas Bee
Ensign George Leecey

Privates:

Joseph Yearns	Aldrick Mires	Bendrick Mires
Benjamin Gregory	James Brown	George Shever
Jacob Ochone	John Oxner	Jeremiah Gregory
Francis Sterling	Richard Harel (90 days)	
John Sneed (90 days)	Thomas Rayburn (90 days)	
Charles Sneed (90 days)		

Additional names, undated and untitled, top and bottom of page illegible.
James Simpson
Captain George Bond

Note: Pat O'Kelley lists the following commanding the Dutch Fork Regiment at Musgrove's Mill:
Captain William Hawsey
Captain Vachel Clary
Captain Humphrey Williamson
Captain William Ballentine
Captain George Stroup
Captain James Wright
Captain William Thompson

Note: Could the men who were paid for 66 days have been wounded at Musgrove's Mill and released from service?

From Clark's *Loyalists in the Southern Campaign, 1981.*

145

APPENDIX II

On the occasion of the State of South Carolina acquiring the Musgrove Mill property, Representative Samuel P. Manning delivered the following address:

MUSGROVE'S MILL, EPIC BATTLE IN THE SUMMER HEAT

By Sam P. Manning

The Battle of Musgrove' Mill August 18, 1780, was one of the epic and classic battles in the American Revolution. It was a battle in which over 300 American volunteers rode thirty miles at night across rugged country, fording five rivers, to attack a British outpost at sunrise and then rode sixty miles in the August heat without stopping for rest. It is a story of adventure, courage, sacrifice, and endurance, an example of patriotism worthy of remembrance. Among the volunteers are many legendary heroes of the nation.

The battlefield which consists of approximately 300 acres on both sides of the Enoree River is in an area of picturesque beauty with rolling hills, thick woods, clean cool streams and river shoals. It is also unique in that it is located in Laurens, Union, and Spartanburg Counties of South Carolina.

After an all night ride from Col. Charles McDowell's Camp on the Broad River in what is now Cherokee County, the American Force reached its destination undetected by the enemy. The Americans were under the command of three Colonels: Isaac Shelby of North Carolina, James Williams of South Carolina, and Elijah Clarke of Georgia. It was half an hour before sunrise. The British forces at Musgrove's Mill were reported by an informant to exceed 500. Col. Innes, a Scotchman, was their Commander.

Capt. Shadrack Inman, a gallant soldier with 25 picked men was selected to attack the British post and to seek to lead the British into an ambush.

The Americans fortified a hilltop in preparation of the fight. Col. Williams commanded the center, Col. Shelby the right and Col. Clarke the left. The Americans were not to be disappointed. A British force was soon chasing Capt. Inman's command at full speed. Across the river, some British soldiers and tories not engaged in the fight climbed to the roof of the Musgrove house which was located on the crest of a hill to watch the chase. In less than an hour to their consternation and shock they saw the forces of the King fleeing pell mell across the Enoree River shoals, the American force in hot pursuit.

Capt. Inman was successful in his mission but paid with his life. After an hour of hard fighting, the Americans were victorious. The British losses were sixty-three killed, ninety wounded, and seventy captured. The American lost were four killed including the brave Capt. Inman and nine wounded.

Isaac Shelby, who was also a hero of Kings Mountain, was quoted in later life as saying that Musgrove's Mill was the hardest fought battle in which he was ever engaged. He credited this to the number of experienced officers who volunteered for the fight.

The American force however could not rest with their victory. At the moment of success a courier arrived notifying them of the American defeat at Camden. Not waiting to rest, the Americans rode sixty miles into the security of the Blue Ridge. Col. Clarke returned to Georgia, Col. Shelby to the western mountains, and Col. Williams delivered the seventy prisoners to Hillsboro, North Carolina.

Musgrove's Mill was a valuable training ground for the patriot forces, for the future heroes of Kings Mountain and Cowpens, two victories which helped make Yorktown possible.

Among the heroes of Musgrove's Mill were men who would serve South Carolina, North Carolina, Georgia, Tennessee, Kentucky and Missouri with honor and great distinction. Among their numbers were future Governors of Kentucky and Georgia and Congressmen from South Carolina, Georgia and North Carolina. Heroes of the nation, fifteen counties in ten states commemorate their memory.

Col. James Williams, a former member of South Carolina's Provincial Congress was promoted to Brigadier General after Musgrove's Mill. He died a hero's death at Kings Mountain. Some of the men in his command were Capt. William Smith who later served in Congress from South Carolina and Lt. Samuel Farrow who represented South Carolina in Congress and as a member of the legislature in 1818 introduced the legislation providing for the state hospital and a school for the deaf and blind. Others included Col. Thomas Brandon later a general in the state militia, Col. Steen, Col. Roebuck, Major Joseph McJunkin and Capt. John Barry, the husband of the Revolutionary heroine, Kate Barry.

Col. Elijah Clarke of Georgia is regarded by historians as Georgia's most famous partisan leader in the Revolution, and one of her most famous Indian fighters. After the Revolution he was a Major General in the Georgia Militia. Counties in Alabama, Georgia, Iowa, and Mississippi commemorate his memory. His son, John Clarke, fought in the battle in his father's command and later served as Governor of Georgia. Governor John Clarke retired to Florida in the 1820's. Major Samuel Hammond of Clarke's command was later promoted to a General in the Georgia Militia, represented Georgia in Congress and was appointed by President Thomas Jefferson as the first Military and Civil Officer for the Upper Louisiana Territory, which was later named the Missouri Territory. Hammond was the first President of the Territorial Council of Missouri. In the 1820's he moved back east to South Carolina and was elected to the State Legislature and then Secretary of State for South Carolina. General Thomas Sumter with whom he had fought in many Revolutionary battles was his strong supporter.

Major Joseph McDowell of North Carolina served with Shelby's command. McDowell was also a hero of Kings Mountain and Cowpens. He was later promoted to General in the North Carolina Militia and was a member of Congress from the state. McDowell County in North Carolina is named in his honor and in honor of his family. With Major McDowell was Capt. David Vance of North Carolina whose grandson was the famous Zeb Vance of North Carolina. Also in Shelby's command was Capt. Valentine Sevier, a brother of Col. John Sevier, the first Governor of Tennessee. Both Governor Vance and Governor Sevier represent their respective states in the Hall of Heroes in the Rotunda of the National Capitol in Washington, D.C.

Col. Isaac Shelby served in both the Virginia House of Burgesses and the North Carolina State Legislature. When Kentucky was created, he was elected its first Governor. Shelby was elected Governor again during the War of 1812, and raised a command of 4000 State Militia which he led in the battle of the Thames in Canada. For his gallant services he was awarded a gold medal from the Congress of the United States. It was Governor Shelby who first created the tradition of the Kentucky Colonel by appointing those who had served under his command in the war, "Kentucky Colonels" on his staff. Counties in Alabama, Illinois, Iowa, Kentucky, Missouri, Ohio, Tennessee and Texas commemorate Isaac Shelby's memory. He was a man who served his country for over a half century with great distinction.

The battlefield at Musgrove's Mill is also famous as having the waterfall on Cedar Shoals Creek where the legendary scout "Horse Shoe" Robinson hid and where the famous heroine Mary Musgrove brought him information and food.

The area of the battlefield is also of interest because it includes "an old Indian field" and a site between Cedar Shoals Creek and the Enoree River where the Colonial Militia of the district had their muster ground. At this site in August 1775, Rev. William Tennant, the famous Presbyterian Divine and fighter for religious freedom and independence who later served as Chief justice of the State explained to the local citizenry and Col. Fletchall' command the Colony's complaint against the Crown. Col. Fletchall commanded the militia of the district. Tennant and Drayton came as representatives of the South Carolina Council of Safety. Col. Fletchall and some of his Tory compatriots insisted on also reading to the audience an address to his people from King George III. It was an interesting confrontation, but there was no violence. Some of the audience sided with the cause of Independence. No doubt their number included James Williams who was later elected to the Provincial Congress from the district. Col. Fletchall remained faithful to the Crown. Another supporter of the King was Capt. Robert Cunningham who later served as a Brigadier General in the Royal Forces in the Revolution. Some after the meeting some of Fletchall's command due to his sympathies organized the Spartan Regiment under the command of Col. John Thomas. After the Revolution the Spartan District named in honor of the Regiment included most of the present Spartanburg and Union Counties and part of Cherokee. Col. Benjamin Roebuck commanded the second Spartan of Fairforest Regiment in the Battle of Musgrove's Mill. Spartanburg County commemorates the valiant Spartan Regiments of the Revolution.

(From the private papers of Dr. George Fields. Used with permission.)

APPENDIX III

Members of the Spartanburg County Commission

Donny Wilder, Former SC Representative from Clinton
Jim Bryan, Former Senator from Laurens County
Ken Driggers, Former Director of the Palmetto Conservation Foundation
Henrietta Morton, South Carolina Society Daughters of the American
   Revolution
Dr. George Fields, Military Heritage Director, Palmetto Conservation
   Foundation

South Carolina Parks Recreation and Tourism Staff

Charles Harrison, State Park Service Director (1991-1999)
Van Stickles, State Park Service Director (1999-2005)
S. Phillip Gaines, State Park Service Director (2005-present)
Mike Foley, Chief of Resource Management (retired)
Frank N. Stovall, Musgrove Mill SHS Park Manager (2000-2008)
John W. Samples, Musgrove Mill SHS Park Technician (2001-2005)
Brodie Davis, Mountain Region Maintenance Chief
Woody Goodwin, Croft State Park

South Carolina Parks Recreation and Tourism Team

The following people helped to physically build the visitor center, the road into the park, the manager's residence, install infrastructure, etc.:

Kurt Becht	Dennis Braswell	Michael Brown
Algie Campbell	Mike Clark	Gene Cobb
David Duke	Jerry Ehmke	
Chester Lawson	Kelly Leitner	Darryl Moore
Robert Padgett	Tom Philyaw	Wayne Schumpert
John Smith	Tod Spaeth	Chip Tiller
John Toby	Rhett Vereen	Jackie Wooten

BIBLIOGRAPHY

Babits, Lawrence. (1998). *A Devil of a Whipping: The Battle of Cowpens.* Chapel Hill: The University of North Carolina Press.

Buchanan, John. (1997). *The Road to Guilford Courthouse: The American Revolution in the Carolinas.* New York, NY: John Wiley & Sons, Inc.

Charles, Tommie. (2010). *Discovering South Carolina's Rock Art.* Columbia, SC: The University of South Carolina Press.

Childs, Bessie Springs. (1911) *"Story of Musgrove's Mill"* pp. 61-63. *Upper South Carolina Genealogy and History, Vol. XXIII, No. 2* May, 2009.

Clark, Murtie June. (1981) *Loyalists in the Southern Campaign.* 3 vol. Baltimore.

Clement, Christopher. (2008). *Data Recovery at Two Sites on Fort Jackson, Richland County, South Carolina.* Columbia, SC: South Carolina Institute of Archaeology and Anthropology.

Clinton, Henry. (1954). *The American Rebellion: Sir Henry Clinton's Narrrative of His Campaign.* (W.B. Wilcox, editor). New Haven, CN: Yale University Press.

Davis, Robert S. (2007). *"Elijah Clarke:Georgia's Partisan Titan."* In *Southern Campaigns of the American Revolution, Vol. 3 No. 3, 38-40.*

Dixon, Max. (1976). *The Wataugans.* Johnson City, TN: The Overmountain Press.

Draper, Lyman. (1881). *King's Mountain and its Heroes.* Reprinted by The Overmountain Press, Johnson City, Tennessee, 1996.

Edgar, Walter. (1998) *South Carolina: A History.* Columbia, SC: The University of South Carolina Press.

Edgar, Walter. (2001). *Partisans and Redcoats.* New York: William Morrow.

Fagan, Brian M. (1987). *The Great Journey: The Peopling of Ancient America.* London: Thames and Hudson.

Fanning, David. *Col. David Fanning's Narrative of His Exploits and Adventures as a Loyalist of North Carolina in the American Revolution.* Ed. A. W. Savary. Toronto, Ontario: *Canadian Magazine,* 1908.

Frierson, John L. (2000). *South Carolina Prehistoric Earthern Indian Mounds.* A document prepared for the Degree of Master of Arts in History. Department of History. The University of South Carolina.

Goodyear, Albert C. (2005). *"Evidence for Pre-Clovis Sites in the Eastern United States."* pp.103- 112. **Paleoamerican Origins Beyond Clovis.** Texas A&M University Press.

Graves, William T. (2002). *James Williams: An American Patriot in the Carolina Backcountry.* Lincoln, NE: iUniverse. Inc.

Graves, William T. (2012). *Backcountry Revolutionary: James Williams (1740-1780) with source documents.* Lugoff, SC: Southern Campaigns of the American Revolution Press.

Hammond, Samuel. In Joseph Johnson *Traditions and Reminiscences Chiefly of the American Revolution in the South.* Charleston, SC: Walker and James, 1851.

Hays, Louise F. (1946) *Hero of Hornet's Nest: A Biography of Elijah Clark 1733 to 1799.* New York, NY: The Hobson Book Press.

Hiatt, John. (2000). *Historic Resource Study Musgrove Mill State Historic Site.* Columbia, SC: South Carolina Department of Parks, Recreation and Tourism.

Hill, William. (1921) *Col. William Hill's Memoirs of the Revolution* Columbia, SC: The Historical Commission of South Carolina., ed. A. S. Salley, Jr.
    The Memoirs of William Hill are also on the website revwarapps.org under William Hill (SCX1)

Hope, Wes. (2003) *The Spartanburg Area in the American Revolution.* Spartanburg, SC: Altman Printing Company, Inc.

Lambert, Robert S. (1987). *South Carolina Loyalists in the American Revolution.* Columbia, SC:University of South Carolina Press.

Landrum, J.B.O. (1897). *Colonial and Revolutionary History of Upper South Carolina.* Greenville, SC: Shannon & Co., Printers and Binders.

Lawson, John. (1709). *A New Voyage to Carolina.* Reprinted 1967 Chapel Hill : The University of North Carolina Press.

Logan, John H. (1859). *A History of the Upper Country of South Carolina from the Earliest Periods to the Close of the War of Independence. Vols. I & II.* Reprinted 2009. Spartanburg, SC: The Reprint Company, Publishers.

McJunkin, Joseph. *"Memoir of Joseph McJunkin of Union".* in *The Magnolia or Southern Apalachian,* January, 1843, New Series-Vol. II.

Joseph McJunkin's pension application is on
revwarapps.org. (S18118).

McKenzie, Roderick. (1787) in *Strictures on Lt. Col.
Tarleton's History Of the Campaigns of 1780 and 1781 the
Southern Provinces of North America.* London.

Merriweather, Robert L. (1940) *The Expansion of South
Carolina 1729-1765.* Kingsport, TN: Southern Publishers,
Inc.

Morrell, Dan L. (1992). *Southern Campaign of the
American Revolution.* Baltimore, Maryland: The Nautical
and Aviation Publishing Company of America.

O'Kelley, Patrick. (2004). *Nothing but Blood and
Slaughter, Volume Two, 1780.* Booklocker.com. Inc.

Ramsey, David. (1809). *The History of South Carolina.*
Charleston, SC.

Rauch, Steven J. (2005). *"An Ill-timed and Premature
Insurrection" The First Siege of Augusta, Georgia, Sept.
14-18, 1780. Southern Campaigns of the American
Revolution.* Vol. 2 No. 9.

Savage, Henry, Jr. (1968). *River of the Carolinas: The
Santee.* Chapel Hill, NC: The University of North Carolina
Press.

Schenck, David. (1889*). North Carolina 1780-1781: Being
a History of the Invasion of the Carolinas by the British
Army under Lord Cornwallis in 1780-1781.* Raleigh, NC:
Edwards & Broughton, Publishers. (Reprinted by Heritage
Books, Inc., Bowie, Maryland in 2000)

Scoggins, Michael C. (2005). *The Day It Rained Militia:
Huck's Defeat and the Revolution in the South Carolina*

Backcountry May -July 1780. Charleston, SC: The History Press.

Shelby, Isaac. (1814). ***Isaac Shelby's Account of his Exploits During the Revolutionary War.*** Shelby and Hart Collection #659z in the General and Literary Manuscripts, Manuscripts Department, Wilson Library, The University of North Carolina at Chapel Hill.

Stokesbury, James L. (1991). ***A Short History of the American Revolution.*** New York: William Morrow and Company, Inc.

Swager, Christine. (2008). ***Heroes of Kettle Creek: 1779-1782.*** West Conshohocken, PA: Infinity Publishing.

Tarleton, Lieutenant-Colonel (Banastre). (1787*).* ***A History of the Campaigns of 1780 and 1781 in the Southern Provinces of North America.*** Reprinted in 2005. Cranbury, NJ: The Scholar's Bookshelf.

White, Max E. (2002). ***The Archaeology and History of the Native Georgia Tribes.*** Gainsville, FL: University Press of Florida.

Williams, James. (1780). ***"Williams' Report on the battle of Musgrove Mill."*** In Graves, William (2012). ***Backcountry Revolutionary.*** pp.196-197. Camden, SC: Southern Campaigns of the American Revolution Press.

Young, Thomas. (1843). ***"Memoir of Major Thomas Young, A Revolutionary Patriot of South Carolina."*** Orion.

INDEX

Index

Gowen's Old Fort, 31, 32, 50,
73, 90, 125
Graves, Will, i, 42, 43, 44, 45,
56, 67, 72, 80, 156, 159
Great Wagon Road, 15
Green, Val, ii, 8, 13, 102
Greene, McKeen, 104
Greene, Nathanael, 85, 86, 89,
94, 95
Grindal Shoals, 36, 86

H

Hammond, Samuel, 48, 56, 58,
59, 61, 62, 65, 68, 69, 104,
122, 148, 157
Hampton, Capt. Edward, 78
Hart, Oliver, 26, 159
Hayes, Joseph, 93, 95, 100
Henderson, Robert, 80, 104
Hill, William, 44, 45, 79, 80,
110, 143, 153, 157, 158, 159
Holman, Jacob, 105
Huck's Defeat, 53, 73, 89, 90,
159
Hughes, David, 105, 106
Hughes, Joseph, 105

I

Inman, Shadrick, 58, 62, 68, 69,
92, 105, 135, 138, 147
Innes, Alexander, 52, 53, 58,
60, 66, 69, 73, 117, 126, 146

J

Jenkins, John, 94
Jones, John, 31, 66, 143

K

Kenedy, William, 105
Kennedy, WIlliam Pendleton,
71, 114, 115, 116, 117, 118,
132, 141
Kentucky, vii, 40, 42, 112, 148,
149
Kerr, James, 52, 53, 54
Kershaw, Joseph, 26
Kettle Creek, 2, 29, 37, 61, 75,
85, 94, 159
King's Mountain., iii, vii, 90,
95, 105, 118, 126, 127

L

Landrum, Dr. J. B. O., i, 93,
121, 122, 157
Laurens, 42, 80, 105, 133, 135,
136, 146, 151
Lawrence, Isaac, 105, 106, 144,
153
Lawson, John, 4, 8, 9, 151, 157
Lawson's Fork, 4, 33
Lindsay, Moses, 106
Little River, 34, 42, 44, 45, 78,
80, 93, 95
Little River Militia, 42, 80, 93,
95
Logan, John, 19, 63, 64, 69, 79,
118, 119, 120, 121, 157
Long Cane Militia, 37
Lumpkin, Dr. Henry, 122, 123,
124, 125, 126
Lyle, Pelham, 120

M

MacKenzie, Roderick, 52, 53,
84

161

Index

CPSIA information can be obtained
at www.ICGtesting.com
Printed in the USA
FFHW011350120219
49930234-55774FF